ATONEMENT AND VIOLENCE

ATONEMENT AND VIOLENCE

A Theological Conversation

EDITED BY JOHN SANDERS

Abingdon Press
Nashville

ATONEMENT AND VIOLENCE
A THEOLOGICAL CONVERSATION

Copyright © 2006 by Abingdon Press

This book is printed on acid-free paper.

Library of Congress Cataloging-in-Publication Data

Atonement and violence : a theological conversation / edited by John Sanders.
    p. cm.
Includes bibliographical references and index.
ISBN 0-687-34294-5 (binding: pbk. : alk. paper)
1. Atonement.   2. Violence—Religious aspects—Christianity.
3. Nonviolence—Religious aspects—Christianity.   4. Jesus Christ—Crucifixion.   5. Sacrifice—Christianity.   I. Sanders, John, 1956-

BT265.3.A86 2006
232'.3—dc22

2006008522

06 07 08 09 10 11 12 13 14 15—10 9 8 7 6 5 4 3 2 1

MANUFACTURED IN THE UNITED STATES OF AMERICA

CONTENTS

CONTRIBUTORS

Hans Boersma is the J. I. Packer Professor of Theology at Regent College, Vancouver, British Columbia. He is the author of *Violence, Hospitality, and the Cross: Reappropriating the Atonement Tradition*.

T. Scott Daniels, PhD, is Senior Pastor at Pasadena First Church of the Nazarene in California. He is the author of the forthcoming *To the Angel, Write: Seven Spirits that Destroy the Church*.

Thomas Finger is an independent scholar who does a great deal of work with Mennonite organizations such as Mennonite World Conference. He is the author of *A Contemporary Anabaptist Theology: Biblical, Historical, Constructive*.

John Sanders is Visiting Professor of Religion at Hendrix College in Conway, Arkansas. He is the author of *The God Who Risks: A Theology of Providence*.

J. Denny Weaver is Professor Emeritus of Religion and Harry and Jean Yoder Scholar in Bible and Religion at Bluffton University, Bluffton, Ohio. Among his publications are *Becoming Anabaptist: The Origin and Significance of Sixteenth-Century Anabaptism*, *Teaching Peace: Nonviolence and the Liberal Arts* (edited with Gerald Biesecker-Mast), *The Nonviolent Atonement*, and *Keeping Salvation Ethical: Mennonite and Amish Atonement Theology in the Late Nineteenth Century*.

Introduction

John Sanders

When we get to the doctrine of atonement in my theology class, I begin by saying: "I am going to role-play a person who is interested in learning more about Christianity, so please tell me the gospel." Since most of my students are from Christian backgrounds they are eager to demonstrate that they know what the gospel is. They typically tell me that we are sinners and thus guilty before God. However, God sent his Son to die for us so that we might be forgiven. I then play Socrates and ask a number of questions that, after twenty minutes or so, have the students totally exasperated with their inability to answer the questions in a satisfactory manner. For instance, I say, "What you are saying is that if I place my trust in the work of Jesus then I am completely forgiven and I do not have to follow Jesus after that." They respond by saying that atonement involves more than mere forgiveness but they are at a loss to explain what that more entails. The point of this exercise is to show them that the "simple gospel" is not quite as simple as they had thought and to help them be open to ways of explaining the gospel that they have never before encountered.

I then go on to say something like the following. Christians have always agreed that Jesus is the savior. They have not, however, always agreed on the way in which to understand just how Jesus saves. The New Testament writers used a wide array of images and conceptual metaphors to convey the gospel message. Later on, major models or theories of the atonement were developed in order to articulate the meaning of the atonement in ways that would resonate with the cultural ethos of the day. Certain aspects of these models seemed strange or even scandalous to later Christian thinkers and so revisions were made to previous theories or entirely new ones were developed. Though no "orthodox" view of the atonement has ever been developed by Christians, for there has never been an ecumenical council on the topic, certain views have gained de facto supremacy at various times in church history.

The penal view, favored in Western Christianity since the Reformation, holds that Jesus died for us by taking the punishment we deserved. He suffered the violence that was due us. In 2004, Mel Gibson's film *The Passion of the Christ* depicted his understanding of that violence in graphic detail. Many viewers were quite moved by the movie as they reflected on what Jesus went through on their behalf. One viewer said, "I'll never take communion the same way again. I knew he suffered for my sake but I did not know how much." Other viewers, however, were put off or offended by the film, wondering how God could ever desire that sort of violence. The film did not create this controversy about God's involvement with violence; it simply served to highlight the divergent perspectives Christians have on the subject.

As mentioned above, later Christians have critiqued the models of atonement favored by earlier generations. It should not surprise us that certain elements of the penal model now seem strange or scandalous to some contemporary Christians. They are asking questions about the nature of the God we worship. Does God have to punish sinners? Did God want the violence perpetrated on Jesus? Was it part of the divine plan of redemption? If so, is God inherently violent? If violence is part of the Christian gospel does this justify particular acts of violence by Christians? From Roman Catholic to Mennonite, United Methodist to Presbyterian, and evangelical to mainline, theologians are once again busy rethinking the atonement of Christ, and one of the main reasons for this reconsideration involves the issue of violence.

Our worship and the very way we explain the gospel are often couched in terms involving violence. Moreover, atonement theology has played an important role in shaping our societal structures and personal relationships. Consequently, some critics allege that many of our society's problems are, in part, a result of faulty conceptions of atonement and their attending notions of God. These critics trace the shortcomings of our criminal justice system, the abuse of women, and oppression of minorities to violent understandings of the atonement. They claim that improper views of the atonement help give rise to improper ways of relating to one another. For instance, some allege that the penal model of atonement entails divine child abuse. God the Father enacts violence on the Son in order to satisfy his holy nature: the Father "takes it out" on the Son instead of on us. Furthermore, they charge, if this is the correct way to follow Jesus, then women and children who are victims of violence are mistakenly taught it is their "cross to bear" and the victims are discouraged from standing up against the violence.

As might be expected, other theologians seek to defend or modify our popular conception of atonement from these criticisms. Some defenders argue that the criticisms are based on caricatures of the penal substitution model. Others claim that though some of the criticisms are legitimate, the model can be modified to accommodate these concerns so there is no need to jettison the view. Proponents of this later strategy seek to revise the penal model so that human injustice is not given divine sanction and so victims of violence have theological grounds upon which to put a halt to the abuse.

This book brings together some of the leading voices on both sides of this discussion.[1] The focus of this book concerns God's intention regarding the violence suffered by the Son. If God the Father used the cross of Christ to redeem us, did the Father intend for the Son to experience the violence he did? Is violence necessary for redemption? If the Father did not intend the cross, then does it have any significance for our salvation? Does any connection between Jesus' suffering and redemption valorize suffering? Should we understand suffering as a means to reconciliation with God or as a consequence of our reconciliation? Enmeshed in this debate are diverse understandings of the divine nature, the relationship between divine justice and love, the nature of sin, and ethics. Some Christian traditions highlight the life and resurrection of Jesus more than his death. Other traditions take the reverse position. Was the death of Jesus necessary for atonement? If we focus on his death, do we neglect Jesus' life as an example to follow? The New Testament writers apply the atonement of Jesus to the lives of followers: it is intended to change lives individually and corporately. Consequently, the topic of this book is not merely about the atonement but goes to the very heart of what it means to live as a Christian in today's world.

It is not uncommon for a layperson to ask of theology: "So what? What difference will it make if I affirm one model of the atonement instead of another one?" This is a fair question to pose to our authors. What impact might it have on our worship, especially baptism and communion, if one view is affirmed instead of another? Would it affect the way we relate to one another in a congregational setting? Regarding evangelism, how would a particular model of the atonement communicate the good news? What exactly is the gospel? Is it about being forgiven and not having to feel guilty, or about being reconciled to God and others, or about freedom from evil powers, or about the ability to emulate the values of Jesus? What difference would affirming a particular view of the atonement make in our approach to civil rights, gender, and minority issues? Does it have any implications for economic relations? Should it affect the kinds of things we want our federal government to do in relation to other nations? Should we revise the criminal justice system in our country away from its focus on retributive punishment? These are the sorts of issues being addressed in the contemporary discussion on atonement theology and our authors address them by examining the subject of violence and the atonement.

What exactly is meant by "violence"? In general, our authors agree on a broad definition given by Hans Boersma: "any use of force or coercion that involves some kind of hurt or injury—whether this coercion be physical or nonphysical, personal or institutional, incidental or structural." Clearly this includes harm or damage done to another such as killing or war, but it also includes such things as economic oppression and racism. Questions do arise, however, regarding the extent to which this should be applied. Are we using violence if we forcibly prevent someone from committing suicide? What about a mother grabbing her toddler before he falls into the lake? Do United Nations embargoes on a country employ violence? Are any kinds of boundaries or demarcations inherently violent? For instance, is it violent to categorize people as Hispanic or Asian? What about distinguishing good from poor students? Is the divine separation of sheep from goats a violent act? Our authors wrestle with how to answer such questions. They certainly disagree that the use of violence is always wrong and they disagree as to whether God is ever directly responsible for violence.

Having discussed the definition of violence, we need to examine what is meant by "atonement." The New Testament contains a wide array of images and concepts attempting to convey the meaning of Jesus' life, death, resurrection, and ascension.[2] Some of these are: reconciliation, redemption, justification, forgiveness, new creation, vicarious sacrifice, the Passover lamb, cleansing blood, and victor over evil powers. No single image or conceptual metaphor can possibly say all that needs to be said regarding Jesus' accomplishment over sin and death, so the New Testament writers employed a host of ideas in order to help their audiences grasp something of the atonement in ways that would make sense in their specific cultural contexts.

In the history of the church, a number of views on the atonement have been put forward that attempt to apply some of these New Testament images to changing historical situations.[3] These are commonly referred to as theories of the atonement and include: *Christus Victor*, ransom, satisfaction, penal substitution, moral influence, moral government, scapegoat, and vicarious repentance to name but a few. Textbooks typically highlight four of these theories and they are the primary ones discussed in this book. A brief description of these is in order, though it must be kept in mind that each one has numerous variations.

Christus Victor, especially popular in the second through fourth centuries, understands the work of Christ primarily as overcoming the forces of evil that hold humans in bondage. The powers of evil work through individual humans as well as political and economic social structures to get humans to treat one another in ways contrary to how God would have us live, thus resulting in sin and death. Consequently, humans have become enslaved to these powers and cannot liberate themselves. Jesus, however, by faithfully following the will of God did not become enslaved to the powers of evil. In his battle against evil Jesus is killed and it seems that the forces of evil have won. Through his resurrection, however, Jesus triumphed over the evil powers and works to liberate humans from their enslavement. The resurrection is thus key to our salvation. One important variation of this view is called the ransom model in which it is thought that the devil held humanity captive but Jesus was the ransom price paid, allowing us to return to God.

Anselm of Canterbury (1033–1109) is credited with the development of the second major model, the satisfaction theory. He saw the human predicament in terms of a vassal who has refused to give the king what is due him. By refusing to honor God as we should, we have all become outlaws without legal rights and are justly condemned to death. In medieval society the punishment not only depended on the crime but on the rank of the offended person. Since we have offended the Infinite Being, the offense is so great that we are incapable of restoring the universe to its proper order. Jesus as a human lives a sinless life, thereby giving to God what we are all supposed to give. His sinlessness means that death is not required of him. By his voluntary death Jesus makes reparation for human sins. But how could a finite human repay an infinite debt? Because Jesus was also divine! Hence, his voluntary death was seen as an act of infinite goodness, which satisfied the divine honor, restoring humanity to proper relations with God. Salvation comes through the death of Christ.

Abelard (1079–1142), dissatisfied with both of the preceding views, proposed the moral influence theory. "Moral" influence is a bit of a misnomer for Abelard's version of this view since his focus is really on the influence divine love brings about in our lives.[4] For Abelard, God loves us dearly and wants us back in proper relationship with him and with one another. The cross is not about victory over the devil or satisfaction of a debt or even procuring forgiveness. God loves us and does not hold our sin against us. Though we are in bondage to sin, the way to liberation lies in accepting the divine love and becoming a loving person in turn. Jesus' life and death manifest God's unique act of grace by coming to us, becoming one of us, and living and loving as we were intended. This demonstration of divine love kindles in us a love for God so that we live out of love, not fear. Salvation is simply God's gift of unimaginable love through Jesus.

The medieval penitential system left humans insecure, for they could never be sure, no matter how pious, that God forgave them. John Calvin and other Reformers sought to change this situation, in part, by the development of the penal substituionary model of atonement. According to this model, God's holiness demands that he punish sin. God is not necessarily angry at us, but the righteous judge cannot just let sin go.[5] We justly deserve death and hell as punishment for our sins. God, however, solves the problem himself by sending his Son to undergo the punishment due us. By his suffering and death, Jesus, the substitute, pays our penalty for us. Consequently, we can escape our punishment and be forgiven and justified. In this view, the focus is on his vicarious death on the cross, which provides us assurance that our salvation is complete.

The penal substitution model has become the quasi-orthodox view in Western Christendom since the time of the Reformation and has become popular among Protestants and Catholics alike. Mel Gibson's *Passion of the Christ* depicts his Roman Catholic point of view but it was evangelical Protestants who heavily promoted the film. This is not surprising since, although it is commonly affirmed in many forms of Protestantism, it is among evangelicals that the model is truly regnant. In 1999, *Christianity Today*, the flagship magazine of evangelicalism, published "The Gospel of Jesus Christ: An Evangelical Celebration" containing an explanation of the gospel written by a number of evangelical leaders. One of the statements reads: "Jesus paid our penalty in our place on his cross, satisfying the retributive demands of divine justice by shedding his blood in sacrifice and so making possible justification for all who trust in him."[6] It goes on to assert that any view that rejects the penal substitution theory is incompatible with the gospel. It is this model, however, that has come under particular scrutiny in recent decades, in part because of the connection between God and violence entailed in it.

Some critics go so far as to assert that all views of the atonement, not just the penal model, entail divine complicity in violence and thus must be rejected because they lend legitimacy to the oppression of women and minorities as well as sanction the use of violence by Christians. Some claim that if the atonement is essential to Christianity, then either Christianity itself must be rejected or the atonement must be deleted from Christianity. Others, however, believe that certain models of the atonement can be modified in order to take the critic's concerns into account. The authors of this book take this latter option. Though they each favor a particular model of the atonement, they realize that it must be qualified in light of legitimate criticisms. The authors disagree among themselves as to which model is preferable for coping with the issue of violence. The reader is invited to listen in on a dialogue as our authors work through the issue. First, each author lays out a constructive proposal regarding how best to handle the doctrine in light of the biblical material and contemporary concerns. Then each essay is followed by the comments of the other three contributors, detailing points of agreement and criticisms.

Two of our authors, J. Denny Weaver and Thomas Finger, are from the Anabaptist tradition renowned for its promotion of nonviolence. Of the contributors, Weaver is the most uncomfortable with traditional formulations of the atonement, particularly the satisfaction and penal substitution views. He does, however, find that the *Christus Victor* model can be significantly reworked in order to arrive at a view that, he believes, promotes a nonviolent atonement. In contrast, Finger is more concerned about faithfulness to traditions and is appreciative of the strengths of the various atonement models. Yet he believes that *Christus Victor*, as found in Eastern Orthodoxy and especially in Irenaeus, is the best path to follow in order to help Christians live nonviolently. Hans Boersma represents the Reformed tradition. Boersma is sensitive to the criticisms raised by Weaver and others but he believes the penal substitution model can be revised in a way that renders that model superior for addressing the issue of violence. He does this by modifying the penal view in light of Irenaeus's recapitulation theology. Also, he argues that no view entirely extricates God from violence, broadly conceived, and though we must in certain circumstances resort to violence (again broadly conceived) this does not sanction every form of violence. T. Scott Daniels affirms a contemporary understanding of the atonement based on the work of René Girard.[7] He sees Jesus functioning as the scapegoat, someone upon whom society places the blame and so becomes the object of our violence. Through this event, however, God unmasks our real motives and self-deception. Once unmasked, we are liberated to live in new ways without the violent scapegoating of others.

It is our hope that this book will enhance the theological discussion. For those interested in learning more, a bibliography of books and key journal articles for further reading is included at the end.

Notes

1. See the book-length treatments on the topic by two of our contributors: J. Denny Weaver's *Nonviolent Atonement* (Grand Rapids, MI: Eerdmans, 2001) and Hans Boersma's *Violence, Hospitality, and the Cross: Reappropriating the Atonement Tradition* (Grand Rapids, MI: Baker Academic, 2004). Some readers may wonder why this collection of essays does not include any female voices. The answer is that we greatly desired to do so but, unfortunately, we were unable to obtain a contribution from the women solicited because of constraints on their time.

2. Helpful here is Joel B. Green and Mark D. Baker, *Recovering the Scandal of the Cross: Atonement in the New Testament and Contemporary Contexts* (Downers Grove, IL: InterVarsity Press, 2000), 35-115.

3. For a thorough historical survey see H. D. McDonald, *The Atonement of the Death of Christ: In Faith, Revelation and History* (Grand Rapids, MI: Baker, 1985).

4. The title of Vincent Brümmer's book *The Model of Love* (New York: Cambridge University Press, 1993) better conveys Abelard's intent.

5. Calvin does say at one place that God is angry at us (*Institutes* 1.15.6), but a few pages later (1.16.2) he says that God's "anger" is only an expression intended to help us see our plight. God always loved us, he says, otherwise he would never have sent his Son.

6. "The Gospel of Jesus Christ: An Evangelical Celebration," *Christianity Today* 43, no. 7 (June 14, 1999): 52.

7. An earlier draft of the essay by T. Scott Daniels was originally coauthored with Marty Michelson. However, Daniels is the one who revised the essay for publication and is responsible for the responses to the other essays.

CHAPTER 1

NARRATIVE CHRISTUS VICTOR: THE ANSWER TO ANSELMIAN ATONEMENT VIOLENCE

J. Denny Weaver

Questions of violence and atonement have generated much discussion in the last several years. Classic atonement images have been attacked as violent, and these attacks have provoked efforts to defend standard atonement images. I enter this debate on the side that critiques the violence of traditional atonement images. The argument has two parts. The first part shows that all standard images of atonement have problematic violent dimensions that render them unacceptable. This particular essay focuses primarily but not exclusively on Anselmian, satisfaction atonement. The argument does not deny that Jesus encountered violence. What is at stake is whether that violence is divinely willed and whether God's modus operandi presumes or depends upon violence. Counter to a common methodology of attempting to salvage all atonement motifs and integrate them into a supposedly more complete picture of the significance of the death of Jesus, my argument exposes the divine violence intrinsic to any and all forms of satisfaction atonement, and shows that no amount of redefining or reinterpreting or supplementing or amending or enriching the satisfaction motif overcomes that violence. It should be abandoned.

The second part of the argument is then to construct an alternative motif that is thoroughly nonviolent and that avoids all the errors and problems discernible in satisfaction atonement.[1] This constructive task is actually more than an atonement motif. It is a way of reading the narrative of Jesus, as well as the history of atonement doctrine, with implications far beyond atonement.

The essay uses broad definitions of the terms *violence* and *nonviolence*. *Violence* means harm or damage, which obviously includes the direct violence of killing—in war, capital punishment, murder—but also includes the many forms of systemic violence such as poverty, racism, sexism, and heterosexism. *Nonviolence* also covers a spectrum of attitudes and actions, from the classic Mennonite idea of passive nonresistance through active nonviolence and nonviolent resistance that would include various kinds of social action, confrontations, civil disobedience, and posing of alternatives that do not do bodily harm or injury. The goal of such actions is to reveal injustice and violence in ways that enable change and reform rather than attempting to eliminate injustice and violence by more violence and killing.

Atonement Motifs

The standard account of the history of doctrine lists three families of atonement images. Each atonement image attempts to explain what the death of Jesus accomplished, or in popular language, to explain "why Jesus died for us." But as will become clear in the remarks that follow, it is important to distinguish them as separate and distinct approaches to the question about Jesus' death. Their different approaches appear clearly when we visualize the object or the "target" of the death of Jesus for each family of images.

Christus Victor, the predominant image of the early church, existed in several forms, each of which involved the three elements of God, the devil or Satan, and sinful humankind. In the *ransom* version of *Christus Victor*, the devil held the souls of humankind captive. The devil is thus the target of the death of Jesus, as it becomes the ransom payment that secures the release of captive souls. In the image of a *cosmic battle*, the devil is less clear as a "target." But as will become clear, it is significant to see that responsibility for the death of Jesus ends up with the devil and not elsewhere.

Satisfaction atonement theories exist in several versions with varying emphases. For the argument here, it suffices to sketch two versions. In 1098 Anselm published *Cur Deus Homo,* which constitutes the first full articulation of *satisfaction* atonement. Anselm wrote that Jesus' death was necessary in order to satisfy the offended honor of God. Human sin had offended God's honor and thus had upset divine order in the universe. The death of Jesus as the God-man was then necessary in order to satisfy God's honor and restore the order of the universe. In other words, God, or some formulation of God's honor, is the target of the death of Jesus.

A change in this image of satisfaction occurred with the Protestant Reformers. For them, Jesus' death satisfied the divine law's requirement that sin be punished. Thus with his death, Jesus submitted to and bore the punishment that was really due to us—humankind—as sinners. Jesus was punished in our place. Jesus substituted himself for us, and died a *penal, substitutionary* death. This motif is the most familiar atonement image for the entire scope of evangelical Protestantism. In this motif, it is not God or God's honor that is the target of Jesus' death. Now it is God's law that is the object of the death of Jesus, as the substitutionary death satisfies a provision of the divine law.

The third atonement image is *moral influence.* In this image, the death of Jesus is a loving act of God aimed toward us. God the Father shows love to us sinners by giving us his most precious possession, his Son, to die for us. In other words, the death of Jesus targets "us," sinful humankind, as its objects.

Reviewing the objects or targets of the death of Jesus makes clear that these really are different images. The death flies off in three separate directions—toward Satan, toward God or a God-related entity, and toward us.

Deleting the Devil from Atonement

But visualizing the objects of the death of Jesus does more than just distinguish three families of atonement motifs. These theories did not develop as isolated entities. Visualizing the differing objects of the death of Jesus helps clarify how later ones responded to earlier ones.

In the first book of *Cur Deus Homo*, Anselm specifically rejected the idea that Jesus' death was a ransom payment to the devil. Satan has no contractual rights that would obligate God to make such a payment. And even though humankind deserves punishment, Satan has no right to inflict that punishment. These considerations make it unworthy of God to deal with Satan via a ransom. Thus Anselm deleted the devil from the salvation equation.[2] Rather than seeing human beings as captive to the devil, Anselm made them directly responsible to God. Humans sinned against God; sin offended the honor of God, and thus threatened order in the universe. The death of Jesus served to restore God's honor and thus restore order in the universe. By deleting the devil from the equation, Anselm shifted the target of the death of Jesus away from the devil and toward God. Later Protestantism then shifted the target from God's honor to God's law.

Abelard's school followed Anselm in rejecting the idea of Jesus' death as a ransom payment to the devil. But Abelard also rejected the idea of Jesus' death as a payment to God. Or in my terminology, Abelard rejected God as the object of the death of Jesus. Instead, Abelard saw the death of Jesus aimed at sinful humankind. It was a loving act of God, targeting sinners in order to get their attention so that they could see the love of God for sinners while they were yet sinners.

Two Questions

Visualizing the objects of the death of Jesus raises additional questions that expose the intrinsically violent character of any and all versions of Anselmian satisfaction or penal substitutionary atonement. Note the nuance that appears when we shift from asking about the object of the death of Jesus to inquire, *Who or what needs the death of Jesus?* For the ransom theory, one might say that the devil clearly needs the death—it fulfills God's part of the bargain when the devil releases the souls of humankind. For the cosmic battle image, the question makes little sense. For the two forms of satisfaction, it is God's honor or God's law that needs the death. Without it, the debt to God's honor remains unpaid or unsatisfied, or the penalty required by God's law remains unmet. Finally, for the moral theory, one might say that "we"—sinners—need the death since that is what enables us to perceive the Father's love shown for and to us.

And now more provocatively, observe what happens when one asks, *Who arranges for or is responsible for the death of Jesus?* Or put crassly, *Who ultimately killed Jesus?*

With the two forms of *Christus Victor*, it is obvious that the devil killed Jesus. But God the Father looks particularly bad in the ransom version—handing the Son over for death as a ransom payment to purchase freedom for God's other children, or as a debt payment to Satan, who possesses rights in a contractual arrangement with God. One can easily sense Anselm's distaste for this motif.

But the situation is not ameliorated when one interrogates the satisfaction and moral theories about who arranged the death of Jesus. Satisfaction atonement pictures a debt owed to God's honor. God's honor not only needs the death, God also arranges for Jesus to die to pay the debt to God's honor. It really looks as though God has Jesus killed in order to pay the debt to God's honor. Here is where we very pointedly see the result of Anselm's deletion of the devil from the three-cornered relationship involving the devil, sinners, and God. With Satan deleted, those remaining in the equation are God and the sinners who have offended God. Of these two, sinful human beings cannot save themselves by repaying God, which means that only God remains in the equation as an actor with power or agency to change the situation. Thus it is merely an extension of the interior logic of Anselm's own move of deleting the devil that leads to the conclusion that God is the only actor remaining to orchestrate the death of Jesus in order to pay the debt owed to God's honor.[3] In penal substitution, Jesus is punished by death, in place of killing us. Thus God's law receives the necessary death that it demands for justice. But again, since sinners cannot pay their own debt, God is the one who arranged to provide Jesus' death as the means to satisfy the divine law. Some scholars have attempted to blunt the fact that God needed and orchestrated the death of Jesus by arguing that Jesus submitted voluntarily to the death that would satisfy God's honor or God's law. But stressing the voluntary character of the death does not change or challenge the overall framework in which God is the only powerful actor, one who needs the death to restore honor or the distorted order of creation, or to fulfill requirements of the divine law. God remains in the role of avenger or punisher.

One might ask, "Weren't the devil or the mob or the Romans responsible for killing Jesus?" But answering yes to that question within the framework of satisfaction atonement points to a strange juxtaposition or non sequitur. Jesus, who is innocent and who does the will of God, becomes sin, subject to punishment. And the evil powers who oppose the reign of God by killing Jesus—whether understood as the mob, the Romans, or the devil—are the ones who are actually doing the will of God by punishing Jesus or by killing Jesus to provide the payment that God's honor or God's law demands. The strange implication is that both Jesus and those who kill Jesus would be carrying out the will of God. Asserting that both claims are true is nonsense. Avoiding the implications of such mutually exclusive claims by cloaking them in a category such as mystery, or by claiming that the acts of God are too big for our categories to contain, renders meaningless any attempt to use theology to express Christian faith.[4]

Abelard objected to this theory as one that limited God's capacity to forgive and that made God vengeful. "How cruel and wicked it seems," Abelard said, "that anyone should demand the blood of an innocent person as the price for anything...still less that God should consider the death of his Son so agreeable that by it he should be reconciled to the whole world!"[5] But Abelard's replacement, called the moral theory, really fares no better than the rejected satisfaction theory. Remember that while Abelard rejected the idea that Jesus' death was a payment directed toward God's honor, Abelard agreed with Anselm in removing the devil from the equation. But by directing the death of Jesus toward humanity as an act of love, the result is an atonement motif, in which the Father has one of his children—the divine Son—killed in order to show love to the rest of the Father's children, namely to us sinners.

These observations about the implied role of God the Father in satisfaction and moral atonement motifs help explain why a number of feminist and womanist writers have claimed that atonement theology presents an image of divine child abuse.[6] That charge seemed radical and offensive to some Christians. But the problem does not reside with those feminist and womanist writers. Most fundamentally, the observations about the role of God in satisfaction and moral atonement motifs result from drawing out the implications of Anselm's own move to delete the devil from the atonement equation, leaving God as the only actor with agency in the equation.

The conclusion from our first round of observations about classic atonement doctrines is that they portray an image of God as either divine avenger or punisher and/or as a child abuser, a Father who arranges the death of one child for the benefit of the others. This analysis draws out implications of Anselm's deletion of the devil from the atonement equation. It reveals an atonement motif in which divinely required and sanctioned violence is the basis of Jesus' saving work. The following section follows a quite different route to similar conclusions.

Retribution in Atonement

The various versions of satisfaction atonement function with the assumption that doing justice or righting wrongs depends on retribution. Sin creates imbalance. Satisfaction atonement assumes that the imbalance is righted or balanced by death.

One contemporary version and one historic version of this assumption make clear its presence in satisfaction atonement. The criminal justice system of the United States operates on the principle of retribution. It is assumed that doing justice means to inflict punishment, which is understood as violence. The assumption is that small crimes require small penalties, while a big crime requires a big penalty. The most severe punishment, namely death, is reserved for the most heinous crimes. The assumption that doing justice is equated with punishment appears in the public disapproval when what is perceived as a big crime receives only a "wrist tap" as punishment. With an apparent imbalance between deed and punishment, it seems that justice was not done. The assumption of retributive justice—that doing justice means meting out punishment—is virtually universal among North Americans and throughout much of the world.[7]

The assumption that doing justice means to punish underlies satisfaction atonement, and in particular the image of penal substitutionary atonement. This image assumes the necessity of punishment, with innocent Jesus punished in our place. As our substitute, Jesus bore the punishment we deserve.

The motif of Jesus as the substitute object of punishment, which assumes the principle of retribution, is the particular image that feminists and womanists have found so offensive. It puts God in the role of the one who demands retribution. God punishes—abuses—one of God's children for the sake of the others. And the Jesus of this motif models passive submission to innocent and unjust suffering for the sake of others.

The contemporary assumption of retributive justice has a medieval counterpart in the feudal system. I follow R. W. Southern's description of the feudal system and how Anselm's image reflects his feudal worldview.[8] The feudal world was hierarchical. A lord at the top held the hierarchy together. Stability of the system depended on maintaining the honor of the lord at the top of the hierarchy. An offense against the lord's honor incurred a debt that threatened his authority and thus the stability of the system. In order to restore honor and stability, the debt had to be repaid. Simply forgiving the debt or an inability to collect the debt challenged the honor and authority of the lord to maintain the system.

It is not difficult to see that Anselm's image of the atoning death of Jesus reflects the feudal worldview. Human sin has brought imbalance and disharmony into the universe. The restoration of harmony, order, and balance requires a payment to satisfy the offended honor of God. Anselm understood Jesus' death as the debt payment that satisfied the honor of God, and thus restored balance and order in the universe. However, understanding the logic of satisfaction atonement does not depend on knowing feudalism. As was previously noted, for example, the modern criminal justice system constitutes an arena that assumes and models retribution. There is thus no need to dispute Southern's conclusion that feudal society supplies the motif that Anselm elevated to an ultimate image of the way that God maintains order in the universe.[9] Maintaining order in the universe depends on maintaining the honor of God, which necessitates a debt payment—the death of Jesus—to cover the offense to God's honor that was enacted by human sin.

Although Anselm's understanding of satisfaction atonement differs significantly from penal substitutionary atonement, I have treated them together as two versions of atonement that depict a divine need for Jesus' death and that thus direct the death of Jesus Godward. Although in different ways, each depends on retribution. The conclusion is inescapable that *any and all versions of satisfaction atonement, regardless of their packaging, assume the violence of retribution or justice based on punishment, and depend on God-induced and God-directed violence.*

Ahistorical Atonement

Satisfaction atonement accommodates violence in a third way. It structures the relationship between humankind and God in terms of an ahistorical, abstract legal formula. Thus it concerns a relationship that is outside of human history. Further, when visualizing the birth, life, teaching, death, and resurrection of Jesus, quite obviously satisfaction atonement actually needs or uses only the death of Jesus. These elements—positing a transaction outside of history and involving only the death of Jesus—make satisfaction atonement an image that (with one exception treated below) implies little or nothing about ethics, and contains nothing that would challenge injustice in the social order. It is an a-ethical atonement image—it projects an understanding of salvation that is separated from ethics. That is, salvation in satisfaction atonement does not envision a change of status in history or in life on earth; rather it envisions a change in one's status outside of or beyond this life. This a-ethical orientation makes it quite compatible with exercise of the sword, or with accommodation of slavery and racism. And as will be explained shortly, it actually contributes to one kind of violence in history.

The particular significance of these observations about the ahistorical and a-ethical dimensions of satisfaction atonement appears when they are considered against the backdrop of the so-called Constantinian synthesis. Among other things, the exercise of the sword can represent the change in the status of the church from a contrast to an accommodation of the social order. Whereas before Christians did not wield the sword and pagans did, now Christians wielded the sword in the name of Christ. Rather than defining what Christians did on the basis of what Jesus said or did, the operative norm of behavior for Christians became what was good or necessary to preserve "Christian society." And in determining what was good for society, the emperor rather than Jesus became the test case.[10]

I suggest that satisfaction atonement reflects the church after Constantine that had accommodated the sword rather than the early church, which was primarily a pacifist church. The abstract, ahistorical, a-ethical formula permits one to claim Jesus' saving work while wielding the sword that Jesus had forbidden. Similarly, James Cone, founder of the black theology movement, notes how the abstract formulas allowed slave owners to preach a salvation to slaves that preserved intact the master-slave relationship.[11] In other words, stated generally, satisfaction atonement separates salvation from ethics. In contrast, the atonement motif presented in what follows both reflects the nonviolence of Jesus and understands ethics as an integral dimension of salvation.

We have thus far observed three levels of violence in satisfaction atonement. First, removing the devil from the atonement equation, as did Anselm and Abelard, leaves an image of God who saves by violence, and of an innocent Son who passively submits to that violence. That is, its image assumes God-orchestrated and God-directed violence. Second, satisfaction atonement assumes and depends on the violence of retribution, with God in the role of the one who orchestrates that retribution. Finally, the abstract, ahistorical character of satisfaction does not challenge and indeed accommodates violence and violent practices in the social order.

Modeling Passivity

In addition to these arguments about the inner logic of the satisfaction atonement formulas and the image of God they portray, it is also important to examine the image and role of Jesus in these formulas. The importance of this question appears when Jesus is accepted as a reference point for ethics—whether one thinks in terms of the quickly recited "What would Jesus do?" or a very profound discussion of discipleship.

In satisfaction atonement, Jesus is a model of voluntary submission to innocent suffering. Since the Father needs the death of Jesus to satisfy divine honor, Jesus voluntarily agrees to submit to that violence needed to satisfy the honor of God. Or Jesus voluntarily agrees to undergo the punishment deserved by sinful humankind in order that the demand of divine justice be met. In either case, Jesus is a passive and innocent victim, and his role is to submit to that unjust suffering. Because Jesus' death is needed, Jesus models being a voluntary, passive, and innocent victim who submits to suffering for the good of another.

It is important to underscore for whom these images of Jesus as an innocent and passive victim pose a particular concern. As Joanne Carlson Brown, Rebecca Parker, Rita Nakashima Brock, and others point out, it is an unhealthy model for a woman abused by her husband or a child violated by her father, and constitutes double jeopardy when attached to hierarchical theology that asserts male headship.[12] A model of passive, innocent suffering poses an obstacle for people who encounter conditions of systemic injustice, or an unjust status quo produced by the power structure. A short list of examples includes the segregated South prior to the civil rights movement; the de facto housing segregation that still exists in many places; and military-backed occupation, under which land is confiscated and indigenous residents crowded into enclosed territories called "reservations" in North America, "bantustans" in South Africa, and "autonomous areas" in Palestine. For people in such situations of an unjust status quo, the idea of "being like Jesus" as modeled by satisfaction atonement means to submit passively and to endure that systemic injustice. James Cone linked substitutionary atonement specifically to defenses of slavery and colonial oppression.[13] Delores Williams calls the Jesus of substitutionary atonement the "ultimate surrogate figure," which would validate all the unjust surrogacy roles to which black women have been and still are subjected.[14] Such examples show that atonement theology that models innocent, passive suffering does have a specific negative impact in the contemporary context.[15]

A victim is controlled by forces and circumstances beyond himself or herself. A victim surrenders control to others and accepts the injustice imposed by others. Jesus in satisfaction and substitutionary atonement models victimization. When Jesus of this motif is the model for people who have experienced abuse or exploitation, the model underscores their status as victims. For them, being like Jesus means to continue to submit to unjust suffering, abuse, or exploitation. And it should be obvious that since satisfaction poses an image of submission to oppression, it poses no specific challenge to the acts of those who oppress and exploit.[16]

Emphasizing the passivity in Jesus' atoning work points to another problem with satisfaction atonement. That problem is that it focuses on Jesus' death as the culmination and high point of his life, and with the focus on his death, that particular moment becomes the moment that defines his work. Additional problems accompany the focus on a passive death.

For one, if Jesus' death is the purpose and culmination of his existence, then his life and teaching are rendered peripheral to the task of providing the death required by divine honor or divine law. As was the case with Anselm's *Cur Deus Homo*, it is indeed possible to discuss the saving work of Jesus without mentioning any specifics of his life or teaching at all. Stated another way, the effect if not the intent of focus on Jesus' death as the saving element of his work is to relegate his life (along with his teaching) to an elaborate means of getting him killed, so that the death can fly Godward to satisfy divine honor or divine law.

Second, considering and valuing Jesus' death apart from the story of his life contributes in a major way to portraying it as passive submission to innocent suffering. His death appears much less passive when examined as one particular incident in the context of the entire scope of his life, including his resurrection. As the story is told in the Gospels, his life is assertive and confrontational, as becomes clear in the sketch below of narrative *Christus Victor*.

When the death of Jesus is pictured in the light of his active and activist life, it appears that death is not the culmination. His mission was to make the reign of God visible, which is visible and present in his person and in his teaching and in his life—his acts. Thus the incarnation itself has an activist agenda—to make God's reign present and visible in our history. Seen in this light, the death of Jesus—the cross—is not the goal or the culmination of the story. Jesus' death is the result of faithfully carrying out his mission of making God's rule present in the world. His death was not something desired by God to balance a cosmic equation. Rather it was willed by the forces that were threatened by the presence of the reign of God in our history. The idea of the incarnation is an active, activist idea, *if* the life and teaching of Jesus have any meaning. The passive image of the death of Jesus actually contradicts the activist purpose of the incarnation.

Defenses of Satisfaction

A number of scholars have attempted to defend Anselmian or satisfaction atonement against the kind of critiques just stated. Whereas I treated satisfaction and penal substitutionary atonement as different but parallel atonement motifs, others have attempted to use the difference between these two images to defend or salvage satisfaction atonement. One version of this argument claims that the image of penal substitution so distasteful to feminists and womanists is a distortion introduced by later Protestantism. True satisfaction atonement as articulated by Anselm does not picture an angry God who punishes, but rather an image concerned with a defense of God's honor.[17] Thus the argument goes, the death of Jesus is not about having Jesus bear punishment actually merited by human beings, but about restoring order and harmony in the universe. A similar, common salvage effort accepts some version of satisfaction or penal substitution as biblical while also acknowledging the problems pointed out above, but then develops other themes and emphasizes them to blunt or smooth over satisfaction's problematic dimensions.[18]

A parallel argument claims that the versions of satisfaction atonement harmful to women and children are because of turning "an *aneconomic* order of charity, plenitude, and ceaseless generosity into a merely human economy of debt, lack, and . . . life in the mode of donation and gift."[19] When rightly understood, the argument goes, Jesus' sacrifice is not any kind of transaction involving debt payment but is rather about restoring humanity "to participation in the divine life," and "thus Christ's sacrifice becomes the donation of obedience and praise (the return of love) offered by the son to the Father." This is a "substitutionary" role, as the "Son offers worship" to the Father on our behalf that we cannot offer.[20] Daniel Bell develops this understanding of Anselmian atonement as a response to exploitative capitalism. Jesus' model of refusing to cease suffering, Bell argues, becomes the model that Christians should follow in defeating capitalism.[21]

Such defenses of satisfaction atonement abound, more than can be addressed here individually. However, once one has such defenses in mind, it is not necessary to address each one individually in order to address them as a whole. As long as the death of Jesus is aimed Godward, one cannot avoid either the implication that the powers that killed Jesus perform a service for God or that death is the means through which God enables reconciliation. Whether Jesus' death is a matter of restoring the order of creation or God's honor or holiness, or offering obedience and worship to God, the death is still directed Godward. And that is true for any future efforts to find other emphases and nuances and redefinitions not yet contemplated. Changing the emphasis or definition within the framework of the satisfaction image does not deal with the implication of Anselm's deletion of the devil, which leaves God as the sole actor with agency in the salvation equation. One can distinguish Anselm's language from penal substitution, and one can claim that the death restores obedience and worship rather than restoring honor or paying a debt, *but* it is still death that accomplishes the saving work. And someone still has to kill Jesus in order for honor or worship to be offered to God on behalf of sinners. No amount of nuancing and redefining and reemphasizing this or that element will rescue satisfaction atonement from its intrinsically violent orientation, and from the image of God as the ultimate agent behind the death that satisfies God—because satisfaction in any form retains only God as the actor of agency to engineer the saving act of Jesus.

Bell's use of a refurbished satisfaction occurs in the midst of a critique of capitalism and response to liberation theology and merits much more discussion than the brief treatment here. I resonate with his critique of capitalism and his arguments that the church should be an alternative to the state and that violent resistance to oppression only continues a cycle of violence.[22] However, real problems accompany Bell's application of Anselmian atonement. When he says that the oppressed resist oppression by a "refusal to cease suffering," which is modeled on Jesus' refusal to cease suffering, Bell is simply reflecting the focus on passive submission to suffering and death in Anselmian atonement. Bell tries hard to say that this suffering is genuine resistance and that it is not merely a rationalization of victimization and redemptive suffering. He admits that his case is difficult.[23] Just how difficult and ultimately unconvincing his argument is becomes evident when one sees that narrative *Christus Victor* provides an alternative that answers all the problems posed by satisfaction atonement.

Richard Mouw took an entirely different tack in defending satisfaction atonement against the charges of violence. Mouw acknowledged the intrinsic violence of satisfaction atonement, and that atonement theology can be used to further the suffering of women. His primary defense of satisfaction atonement is to explain why the violence of atonement is not a model for emulation. First, following the analogy of just war theory, it uses only the violence necessary to deal with sin—thus it should not contribute to the excessive violence some women experience. Second, the once-and-for-allness of atonement gives it "a kind of ethical-inimitability corollary," meaning that Jesus is not an ethical model, at least not at the point of submitting to unjust violence. Further, he distinguishes between the redemptive suffering of Jesus and masochistic suffering, which is harmful to women. Finally, Mouw revises punishment to become "wrath." This wrath is then not physical punishment, but the experience of being cursed for sin, which Jesus was already experiencing during his life as he identified with humanity, and experienced most profoundly on the cross as he asked, "My God, my God, why have you forsaken me?" Human beings cannot imitate this experience of the wrath of God.[24] These arguments are then said to absolve God of the image of divine child abuser.

Mouw leaves us with the image of a God who uses violence, and with the claim that the actions of Jesus Christ are not a model for Christians, the people supposedly identified by his name. In other words, Mouw leaves us with a view of Jesus that is not useful for ethics and with images of God and of salvation that many have found offensive, but recasts these problems as supposedly unproblematic. But alongside the issue of separation of Jesus from Christian ethics, one must also wonder if continual contemplation of divine violence that supposedly is not imitated may not have the same kind of impact on psyches that concerns psychologists and parents when impressionable young people immerse themselves in violent movies and violent video games—whether through violent theology or violent entertainment people are being conditioned to accept and eventually to practice violence.

Some writers have appealed to the Trinity to defend satisfaction atonement against the claims that it poses a harmful model for abused or oppressed people. According to this argument, the unity of the Persons of the Trinity means that the Father suffers with the Son. Thus rather than having the Father cause Jesus to suffer, one has God the Father both identifying with the suffering of Jesus and also suffering himself for sinful humankind rather than exercising judgment.[25] However, this appeal camouflages but does not deal fundamentally with the abusive imagery of satisfaction atonement. Returning to the earlier questions about the object of Jesus' death and who needs and arranges the death shows that the death of Jesus is still aimed Godward. This appeal does change the image, however, from the Father abusing the Son to the Father engaging in self-abuse—which might be called divine suicide.

Another trinitarian argument defends divine violence by claiming that the violence of judgment is God's role while Jesus the Son has a different role. Without elaborating, it is sufficient to say here that that argument violates the standard understanding of the relation of the Persons of the Trinity to one another within the Godhead. According to standard interpretation, each Person in some way reveals the fullness of God, and there is nothing in the Godhead or in any of the Persons of the Trinity that is not in the others. Following that logic, it is not possible for God to exercise violence while Jesus is only nonviolent, and if Jesus is nonviolent, then the Godhead is also nonviolent. In particular, this point addresses the argument of Richard Mouw, who assumes the violence of God.

None of this discussion about violence and the image of God in atonement motifs and about Jesus as passive model of innocent suffering matters *if* Jesus' life is not related to what it means to be a Christian, and *if* being saved is a status separated from ethics. However, *if* the life of Jesus is relevant as a norm for ethics and *if* being saved and being Christian have expression in how one lives, then the discussion of image of God and of violence in atonement images and of Jesus as model of passive innocent suffering have profound importance. If we take Jesus seriously as a model and a norm for Christians, and if in his person and in his life Jesus is the presence of the reign of God in our history (this is a statement of incarnation), then how we understand atonement is an image of how God works in the world and how we understand what it means to be a Christian in the world. Satisfaction atonement in any of its forms pictures God as a God whose modus operandi is retributive violence and it presents an image of Jesus that models passive, innocent submission to abuse and oppression. This image of God, this image of atonement, and this image of being a Christian in the world should be abandoned.

Obviously, that conclusion raises a big question. What would I put in its place? I have a suggestion, which can be only sketched here.

Narrative *Christus Victor*

My solution to the atonement question is to restore the devil to the equation. But that restoration is not merely putting Satan back into Anselm's equation. It brings the battle of *Christus Victor* down to earth in the recovery and development of a biblical image that had fallen from view long before Anselm. I have called the result "narrative *Christus Victor*,"[26] which identifies the victory of Christ in terms of the narratives of the Gospels and Revelation while also distinguishing it from classic *Christus Victor*. It is an explicitly nonviolent image, and it avoids all the problems of violence identified with classic atonement and christological imagery.

The twelfth chapter of Revelation features the specific image of a heavenly battle between the forces of Satan, represented by the dragon, and the forces of God led by the angel Michael. This battle follows the birth of a baby who was snatched up to heaven after the dragon tried unsuccessfully to kill him. The image of the baby snatched up to heaven clearly refers to the death and resurrection of Jesus, which means that the woman with a crown of twelve stars is Israel that produced Jesus and then the church. The dragon is called "the Devil and Satan" (Rev. 12:9), but the seven heads, ten horns, and seven crowns identify it as a symbol of Rome. There is here then an image of the reign of God in the person of Jesus confronting the evil of the world, symbolized by Rome—a confrontation that is continued by the life of the church. The so-called cosmic battle is really imagery that gives the cosmic significance of the confrontation *in history* between the Roman Empire and Jesus and his church—narrative *Christus Victor*.

The same interpretation applies to the seven seals in Revelation 6 and 7, which I suggest correspond to the seven imperial regimes between the crucifixion of Jesus under Emperor Tiberius (14–37 CE) and the reign of Domitian (81–96 CE), during whose rule the book likely was written. Each seal contains a symbolic reference to an event during the reign of the corresponding emperor.[27]

The "conquering and to conquer" of seal one is a subtle reference to the crucifixion and resurrection of Jesus, and the emperor rider's failed attempt to conquer Jesus. In seal two, the blood-red horse and threat to take peace from the earth recall the threat to Jerusalem in 40 CE, when Emperor Caligula (37–40 CE) commissioned a statue of himself in the form of a god and ordered an army commanded by Petronius to occupy Jerusalem and to install the statue on the high altar of the temple. Caligula died before that order was carried out, and the city was spared.

Seal three has symbols of famine, which was widespread under Emperor Claudius (41–50 CE), and cross-referenced in Acts 11:28. The double ugly riders and the multiple means of spreading death and destruction in seal four certainly represent Emperor Nero (54–68 CE), whose legendary cruelty still reigns. The vision of the heavenly altar in seal five parallels an eighteen-month break in the succession of emperors in 68–69 CE, when three rivals—Galbo, Otho, and Vitellius—each claimed the imperial crown but did not survive long enough to consolidate power.

The imagery of astronomical collapse and earthly chaos and devastation in seal six has been frequently interpreted as a description of the end of the world. It is not. This imagery actually depicts a mundane event, but one that seemed like the end of the world to those who experienced it. In 70 CE, an army commanded by Titus, son of the reigning emperor Vespasian (69–79 CE), invaded Jerusalem and sacked the city. Images of celestial chaos and terrestrial pandemonium together symbolize the breakdown of order and the feelings of loss and devastation when the army of the occupiers utterly destroyed Jerusalem and the temple.

Opening the seventh seal does not occur until chapter 8. The opening was followed by "silence in heaven for about half an hour" (v. 1). After Vespasian, his son Titus (79–81 CE) had a short reign as emperor. Domitian followed, ruling from 81 to 96 CE. Since the sequence of emperors ends here, it indicates that Revelation was most likely written during the reign of Domitian, with little of note to symbolize during the rule of Titus.

The important point in interpreting the seals is that the worst events in the first century—including the sack of Jerusalem in 70 CE—are not the end of the story. The entirety of chapter 7 also belongs to the sixth seal. Here one encounters the renowned image of the 144,000, which constitutes 12,000 from each of the 12 tribes of Israel. Obviously 144,000 is a symbolic number, obtained by squaring the number 12, which symbolizes Israel, and then multiplying by the large number of 1,000, a biblical number used to mean a very large number. One thousand would have seemed much larger to a first-century reader than to us in the computer age who routinely encounter extremely large numbers. One thousand ought not be read as a number of mathematical precision any more than it is mathematically precise today when a busy person proclaims that she has "a million things to do." The author, John, has provided a symbolic way to display God's people, who descend from Israel, as a boundless multitude.[28]

The vignette of the exceedingly large number of God's people descended from Israel is followed immediately by another "great multitude that no one could count" (v. 9), composed of people from every conceivable nation and tribe and language of the earth. When one understands the symbolic character of 144,000, it should be apparent that the two multitudes are comparable in size—each a symbolic depiction of the people of God, one emphasizing continuity with Israel, the other making the point that no ethnic or national group is excluded from the people of God. They proclaim that "salvation belongs to our God who is seated on the throne, and to the Lamb" (v. 10). In verse 14 the reader learns that this white-robed throng has "come out of the great ordeal" and their robes have been washed "white in the blood of the Lamb" and they are pictured as worshiping God "day and night" while the "Lamb at the center of the throne" protects them. What does it mean that this worshiping throng is juxtaposed with the devastation so graphically depicted in the first scene of seal six?

That chapter 7 is four times longer than the scene of devastation indicates relative importance. More substantively, the juxtaposition of scenes of devastation and celebration displays the rule of God, revealed triumphant in the death and resurrection of Jesus, as victorious over the worst imaginable devastation meted out by the forces of evil—symbolized by Rome. With eyes on the resurrected Jesus as the living and embodied representative of God, those who have come through the "great ordeal" of Rome, including the mayhem and destruction of Jerusalem, can celebrate life in the reign of God, where salvation is found. Here is narrative *Christus Victor.*

Of particular importance is the observation that the victory of the reign of God over the evil symbolized by Rome occurs *nonviolently*, through the life, death, and most significantly, the resurrection of Jesus, and through the witness of the church, which maintains its witness in the face of adversity and death. This victory through the resurrection is obvious in the vignettes of the seals in Revelation 6 and 7 and the heavenly battle of chapter 12. It bears pointing out specifically for the image of the rider on the white horse in chapter 19, which is often appealed to in order to show the supposed violence of God and the ultimately vengeful and violent attitude of God toward evil. I simply note that the rider's robe is dipped in blood *before* the supposed battle and that his name is "The Word of God" (v. 13), which clearly identify the rider as the resurrected Jesus. Then note that there is no actual battle depicted; rather the armies of the kings of the earth are defeated by the sword that extends from the rider's mouth (v. 21), which makes it the word of God and not violence that defeats evil. Ephesians 6:17 and Hebrews 4:12 also use a two-edged sword as an image for the word of God. The vivid image of the rider on a white horse conveys a message about the nonviolence of the reign of God. It is another statement that in the resurrection of Jesus, the victory of the reign of God over evil occurs without violence.

The Gospels present the same story as that told in Revelation, but from a different standpoint. Revelation tells the story of Jesus and the confrontation of the rule of evil by the reign of God from the perspective of the heavenly throne room and the future culmination of the reign of God. The Gospels narrate that same confrontation from the earthly vantage point of the folk who got dust on their sandals as they walked along the roads of Palestine with Jesus. Nonetheless, when Jesus' person embodies God, then his person, life, and teaching are the reign of God confronting the rule of evil in human history.

In Nazareth Jesus announced his mission as one "to bring good news to the poor... to proclaim release to the captives and recovery of sight to the blind, to let the oppressed go free" (Luke 4:18). That is an active, not a passive, mission to make God's reign visible. In Walter Wink's interpretation of Jesus' well-known statements about turning the other cheek, giving the cloak, and going the second mile, these admonitions are activist, nonviolent resistance strategies rather than injunctions to passive submission, as usually interpreted.[29] Past the Sermon on the Mount, there are stories that show Jesus in conversation with women when that is not expected; in these instances he challenged some accepted conventions, and thus raised the status of women. Choosing a Samaritan as a good example in the parable of that name, and the story of Jesus' encounter with the Samaritan woman at the well, confront racism against Samaritans by raising their status. Jesus' teachings show concern for poor people. Jesus cast out demons or healed mental illness and he stilled a storm. These accounts portray dimensions of the authority of the reign of God made visible and present in the teaching or acts of Jesus.

Luke 6:6-11 recounts Jesus' healing of a withered hand. A dominant feature of the story is that the healing occurred on the Sabbath day, in defiance of conventional expectations. And the defiance of expectations was clearly deliberate—Jesus had the man come to a prominent spot where everyone could see him, and he looked "around at all of them," drawing their eyes to him before he acted. This event of restoring the Sabbath to a day of restoration and healing made visible the reign of God.

Other stories in the Gospels have similar features. One of the most striking is often referred to as "the cleansing of the temple." We need not engage in the debate about the nature of the particular offense that Jesus encountered in order to know that he was upset with what he found. He knocked over tables and cracked a whip and chased animals and told the money changers to get out because they had made the house of prayer into a "den of robbers" (Luke 19:46). When placed in the context of his teaching and other actions, this very assertive act of chasing out the money changers, salesmen, and their animals ought not come as a surprise. Nonetheless, it was the event that made the authorities so mad that they started plotting how to kill him. The plot met with success as the Romans, the ultimate political authority of the day, executed Jesus. But as is also well known, the success was momentary. Three days later, God raised Jesus from the dead, a triumph of the reign of God over the worst that the evil powers could do, namely to deny Jesus his existence. When the rule of evil confronted the reign of God in Jesus, the reign of God was victorious in the resurrection of Jesus.

Both the Gospels and Revelation locate the victory of the reign of God on earth and in history—narrative *Christus Victor*—and make quite clear that the triumph occurred not through the sword and military might, but nonviolently through death and resurrection. The intrinsically nonviolent character of the victory eliminates what is usually called "triumphalism of the church." As intrinsically nonviolent, its stance to the other or toward those who differ and are different can only be nonviolent. To be otherwise is to cease to be a witness to the reign of God and to join the forces of evil that oppose the reign of God.

Reading that story in the Gospels shows that Jesus was not a passive victim, whose purpose was to get himself killed in order to satisfy a big cosmic legal requirement or to restore worship to God on our behalf. Rather, Jesus was an activist, whose mission was to make the rule of God visible. And as was suggested above, his acts demonstrated what the reign of God looked like—defending poor people, raising the status of women, raising the status of Samaritans, performing healings and exorcisms, preaching the reign of God, and more. His mission was an activist mission to make the reign of God present in the world in his person and in his teaching, and to invite people to experience the liberation it presented.

And when Jesus made present the reign of God, he was killed by an array of forces that represent the rule of evil. These forces included imperial Rome, which carried ultimate legal authority for his death, with some assistance from the religious authorities in Jerusalem, as well as Judas, Peter, and other disciples who could not even watch with Peter, and the mob that howled for Jesus' death.

As sinners, in one way or another, we are accomplices with those sinful forces that killed Jesus.[30] Jesus died making the reign of God present for us while we were still sinners. To acknowledge our human sinfulness means to confess our participation in the forces of evil that killed Jesus, including their present manifestations in such powers as militarism, nationalism, racism, sexism, heterosexism, and poverty, which still bind and oppress.

But because God is a loving God, God invites us to join the rule of God in spite of the fact that we participated with and are captive to the powers that killed Jesus. We cannot compensate for or undo our participation with the powers that killed Jesus; but God invites us to participate in the reign of God anyway. That participation, despite our guilt for opposing the reign of God, is grace. It is also grace because under our own power we cannot resist and overcome the powers of evil. Only God can do that, and if we are resisting and overcoming, it is because God enables it. One can call that predestination. At the same time, we are free moral agents and we have to make a choice whether to remain in league with the forces that oppose God or to accept God's invitation to join with the reign of God. One can call that free will. Together these two impulses express Paul's paradox of grace: "But by the grace of God I am what I am, and his grace toward me has not been in vain. On the contrary, I worked harder than any of them—though it was not I, but the grace of God that is with me" (1 Cor. 15:10).

God invites us to join the struggle of those seeking liberation from the forces that bind and oppress. This invitation envisions both those who are oppressed and their oppressors. When the oppressed accept God's invitation, they cease collaborating with the powers that oppressed and join the forces that represent the reign of God in making a visible witness against oppression. Although they may still suffer as a result of the struggle, they have ceased being victims who submit willingly to unjust suffering. And when the oppressors accept God's invitation, they cease their collaboration with the powers of oppression and join the forces that represent the reign of God in witnessing against oppression. Thus under the reign of God as depicted in narrative *Christus Victor,* former oppressed and former oppressors join together in witnessing to the reign of God.

Earlier it was indicated how Anselmian atonement correlates with the ecclesiology of Christendom. It is now also possible to say that narrative *Christus Victor* belonged to, and only makes sense when perceived within, the ecclesiological status of the early church in relation to the Roman Empire and the social order. As is clear from the symbolism of Revelation, the church in that setting perceived itself to be different from the empire, to maintain itself as distinct from the prevailing social order. My reconstruction of narrative *Christus Victor* that makes visible the church in Revelation and the life of Jesus in the Gospels simply reflects the status of the church in the first century and beyond. I note without elaboration that this church was a pacifist church whether that stance was because Christians did not wield the sword and shed blood or because of the idolatrous nature of the army's religious commitments.[31]

It was this sense of being distinct from the social order that disappeared with the Constantinian synthesis. And with that accommodation, historical dimensions of narrative *Christus Victor* were no longer true, and cosmic imagery did not match the political reality. Thus eventually the motif I have called narrative *Christus Victor* could fade away without a sense of loss, to be replaced by Anselm's satisfaction motif, which reflected the medieval social and ecclesiological conditions.

This essay has used material from the Gospels and Revelation, the two ends of the New Testament. Some readers will no doubt suggest that the writings of Paul tell a much different story and provide a reading in line with satisfaction atonement. I disagree, although I do recognize that one can certainly read Paul in line with Anselmian or satisfaction language. But my argument is that this is not the only reading of Paul, and that Paul can be read just as well within the trajectory of narrative *Christus Victor* that goes from the Gospels to Revelation. Space permits only one brief example, the text of Romans 3:24-26, which is often suggested as proof of Paul's satisfaction orientation. It reads:

> They are now justified by his grace as a gift, through the redemption that is in Christ Jesus, whom God put forward as a sacrifice of atonement by his blood, effective through faith. He did this to show his righteousness, because in his divine forbearance he had passed over the sins previously committed; it was to prove at the present time that he himself is righteous and that he justifies the one who has faith in Jesus.

First, I have been helped by J. Christiaan Beker and Raymund Schwager, who read Paul in apocalyptic and nonsacrificial perspectives.[32] Second, recall that the sacrifices of Leviticus happen in times of joy as well as failure, and therefore cannot be interpreted as rituals that required blood as the necessary payment for sin. Thus even if "sacrifice of atonement" is modeled on Old Testament sacrifices, it need not be read in an Anselmian manner. Sacrifice can be understood as a self-giving without it being any kind of payment or restoration of honor or worship to God. However, Jesus' faithfulness even unto death did reveal his righteousness, and the result of this self-giving death was reconciliation between God and sinners, when sinners come to accept God's invitation to join freely—that is, through grace—the reign of God. And as noted above, when God accepts that sinner into the reign of God, sins are certainly passed over, by grace, and the sinner's faith in Jesus reconciles that sinner to God.

The image of narrative *Christus Victor* avoids all the problematic elements in classic atonement images, particularly those of satisfaction atonement. In contrast to the focus on death in satisfaction atonement, depicting the reign of God as made visible by Jesus in narrative *Christus Victor* requires use of the entire life and teaching of Jesus, culminating with the resurrection. The culmination of Jesus' work in death versus in resurrection makes clear one of the significant differences between satisfaction atonement and narrative *Christus Victor*.

Narrative *Christus Victor* is grounded in assumptions of nonviolence—the nonviolence of Jesus—rather than violence. Earlier questions posed of atonement motifs were, "Who needed the death of Jesus?" and "Who arranged for the death of Jesus?" Posing these questions of narrative *Christus Victor* brings to the foreground the profound difference between it and satisfaction atonement. The questions have nonanswers in narrative *Christus Victor*. God is not put in the role of chief avenger or pictured as a child abuser. The death of Jesus meets no divine requirement because narrative *Christus Victor* does not rest on the idea of retribution where death makes right the problem, however the problem is defined. In narrative *Christus Victor*, the death pays God nothing and is not Godward directed. And thus there is no basis for God to arrange to have Jesus die or be killed to restore something to God. Death is rather what the forces of evil—"the devil"—do to Jesus. Rather than a divine requirement, the death of Jesus is the ultimate contrast of methodology between the reign of God and the reign of evil.

Jesus did suffer and die a violent death, but the violence was neither God's nor God directed. Suffering and dying were not the purpose or goal of Jesus' mission. Death resulted when Jesus faithfully carried out his life-bringing and life-affirming mission to make the rule of God present and visible. Since saving his life would have meant abandoning his mission, his death was necessary in the sense that faithfulness required that he go through death. However, even when Jesus' death was necessary in that sense, death was neither the goal nor the purpose of his life. Perhaps one can understand how death was a by-product of faithfulness rather than the goal of his actions when one recalls the murder of Martin Luther King Jr. King anticipated his death and was killed because of his work, but getting killed was in no way the purpose of his work. Surrendering to fear and saving his life would have meant abandoning his life's work.

I want to make very clear here that I am not denying that Jesus was killed, nor am I removing his death from the Gospel story. Rather I have suggested a different understanding of the role of Jesus' death in the story of salvation, and a different understanding of whose violence killed Jesus.

I am arguing that his death was not willed or needed by God. His death did not pay off or satisfy anything. On the contrary, it was a product of the forces of evil that opposed Jesus and opposed the reign of God. The real saving act of and in and with Jesus is his resurrection.

Narrative *Christus Victor* understands Jesus as the one whose person and mission make the reign of God present in our history. It pictures Jesus with an activist mission, as a model of liberation. Those who accept the invitation of God join the movement that witnesses to the nature of the reign of God in contrast to the forces of evil that bind. This motif thus features salvation that begins in history to the extent that the reign of God is present in history.

Conclusion

This essay has demonstrated the extent to which presuppositions of violence as well as overt violence are intrinsic to supposed standard Christian theology, both through failure to challenge violence and through actual accommodation of violence and injustice. This combination of intrinsically violent elements and lack of challenge to injustice in the social order mean that it has been possible throughout much of Christian history for Christians to profess allegiance to Jesus and to claim salvation as depicted in classic Christology and atonement while simultaneously pursuing the violence prohibited by Jesus' teaching and life.

If Christians are uncomfortable with Christianity as a violent religion—and currently there seem to be many supposedly Christian voices joining the national war chorus—the first step is to recognize the extent to which formulas of classic theology have contributed to violence both overt and systemic. This essay provides some data for that acknowledgement. The second step away from Christianity as a violent religion would be to construct theology that specifically reflects the nonviolence of its namesake, Jesus Christ. As a suggestion I offer narrative *Christus Victor* as both nonviolent atonement and narrative Christology. Finally, step three would be to live out the theology of its nonviolent namesake. That commitment challenges every Christian.

Notes

1. The most extensive product of my work on atonement is the book *The Nonviolent Atonement* (Grand Rapids, MI: Eerdmans, 2001). The essay in hand draws on that book.

2. Anselm, "Why God Became Man," in *A Scholastic Miscellany: Anselm to Ockham*, ed. and trans. Eugene R. Fairweather, The Library of Christian Classics (Philadelphia: Westminster, 1956), 107-10.

3. Anselm himself did not deal with the specific question of whether God was responsible for the death of Jesus, although he does discuss whether the Father willed the death of the Son. Anselm wanted to portray the necessity of the incarnation and of Jesus' death as a payment to God's honor, but without appearing to place limits or obligation on God. To deal with this dilemma and to absolve God of responsibility for seemingly unjust acts, Anselm developed the category of "fitting" or "fittingness" to describe what was necessary for God but without placing necessity or obligation on God. R. W. Southern, *Saint Anselm: A Portrait in a Landscape* (Cambridge: Cambridge University Press, 1990), 201-2, 206. For Anselm's use of "fitting" and "unfitting," see Anselm, "Why?" 115-21.

4. The question of who killed Jesus and the image of God the answer implies play prominently throughout James Carroll's important book on the theological roots of anti-Semitism. Carroll notes that Constantine shifted the focus from resurrection to the death of Jesus as the saving event, which set in motion the dynamic that made "the Jews" the focus of Christian hatred through the centuries. A kind of theological culmination was reached with Anselm's *Cur Deus Homo*, in which Anselm sought to prove the necessity of incarnation and the death of Jesus by reason alone. With Boso as a stand-in for Jews, Anselm thus rendered Jews unreasonable or irrational. As a result, Jews ended up as both unreasonable for rejecting the saving death of Jesus and as the ones who were blamed for providing the event that makes Christian salvation possible. See comments throughout James Carroll, *Constantine's Sword: The Church and the Jews: A History* (Boston: Houghton Mifflin, 2001), especially 54-56, 190-94, 284-89.

5. Peter Abailard, "Exposition of the Epistle to the Romans," in *A Scholastic Miscellany*, 283.

6. Joanne Carlson Brown and Rebecca Parker, "For God So Loved the World?" in *Christianity, Patriarchy and Abuse: A Feminist Critique*, ed. Joanne Carlson Brown and Carole R. Bohn (New York: Pilgrim Press, 1989), 1-30; Julie M. Hopkins, *Towards a Feminist Christology: Jesus of Nazareth, European Women, and the Christological Crisis* (Grand Rapids, MI: Eerdmans, 1995), 50-52; Rita Nakashima Brock, *Journeys by Heart: A Christology of Erotic Power* (New York: Crossroad, 1988), 55-57; Carter Heyward, *Saving Jesus from Those Who Are Right: Rethinking What It Means to Be Christian* (Minneapolis: Fortress Press, 1999), 151; Delores S. Williams, *Sisters in the Wilderness: The Challenge of Womanist God-Talk* (Maryknoll, NY: Orbis, 1993), 161-67.

7. One of several problems with retributive justice is that it does nothing for the victim or to restore the relationship fractured by the offender. For an analysis of retributive justice, with restorative justice as the suggested alternative, see Howard Zehr, *Changing Lenses: A New Focus for Crime and Justice* (Scottdale, PA: Herald Press, 1990).

8. Southern, *Saint Anselm*, 221-27.

9. Ibid.

10. For the seminal treatment of the changes in the church symbolized by Constantine see John Howard Yoder, "The Constantinian Sources of Western Social Ethics," in *The Priestly Kingdom: Social Ethics as Gospel* (Notre Dame: University of Notre Dame Press, 1984), 135-47; as well as John H. Yoder, "The Disavowal of Constantine: An Alternative Perspective on Interfaith Dialogue," in *The Royal Priesthood: Essays Ecclesiological and Ecumenical,* ed. Michael G. Cartwright (Grand Rapids, MI: Eerdmans, 1994), 242-61; and John H. Yoder, "The Otherness of the Church," in *The Royal Priesthood,* 53-64. H. A. Drake has shown that Constantine himself pursued a policy of tolerance, and that the changes he symbolizes and the move toward enforcing one pre-scribed faith actually occurred in the decades following Constantine. H. A. Drake, *Constantine and the Bishops: The Politics of Intolerance* (Baltimore: Johns Hopkins University Press, 2000).

11. James H. Cone, *God of the Oppressed,* rev. ed. (Maryknoll, NY: Orbis, 1997), 42-49, 211-12.

12. Brown and Parker, "For God So Loved the World?"; Hopkins, *Towards a Feminist Christology,* 50-52; Brock, *Journeys by Heart,* 55-57; Heyward, *Saving Jesus,* 151.

13. Cone, *God of the Oppressed,* 211-12.

14. Williams, *Sisters in the Wilderness,* 60-83, 161-67, 178-99.

15. One of the most explicit examples of innocent suffering for another is the voca-tion of "victim soul," which was a prominent feature of some Catholic religious orders, primarily for women, in the nineteenth and well into the twentieth century. See Paula M. Kane, "'She Offered Herself Up': The Victim Soul and Victim Spirituality in Catholicism," *Church History* 71, no.1 (March 2002): 80-120.

16. One might perhaps argue that the satisfaction atonement demands and models retribution for the victim. However, this retributive justice does nothing to restore the victim. See note 7.

17. Catherine Pickstock pushes this argument the farthest, but Margo Houts and Nancy Duff also use it. See Catherine Pickstock, *After Writing: On the Liturgical Consummation of Philosophy* (Oxford: Blackwell Publishers, 1998), 155-57; Margo G. Houts, "Atonement and Abuse: An Alternative View," *Daughters of Sarah* 18, no. 3 (Summer 1992): 30; Nancy J. Duff, "Atonement and the Christian Life: Reformed Doctrine from a Feminist Perspective," *Interpretation* 53, no.1 (January 1999): 24.

18. For different, recent versions of this approach, see Joel B. Green and Mark D. Baker, *Recovering the Scandal of the Cross: Atonement in New Testament & Contemporary Contexts* (Downers Grove, IL: InterVarsity Press, 2000); William C. Placher, *Jesus the Savior: The Meaning of Jesus Christ for the Christian Faith* (Louisville: Westminster John Knox Press, 2001), 136-37, 142-49; and Colin Gunton, "One Mediator...The Man Jesus Christ: Reconciliation, Mediation and Life in Community," *Pro Ecclesia* 11, no. 2 (Spring .2002): 151-52.

19. Daniel M. Bell Jr., "Sacrifice and Suffering: Beyond Justice, Human Rights, and Capitalism," *Modern Theology* 18, no. 3 (July 2002): 344.

20. Bell, "Sacrifice and Suffering," 345-46; Daniel M. Bell Jr., *Liberation Theology After the End of History: The Refusal to Cease Suffering* (London: Routledge, 2001), 147.

21. Bell, "Sacrifice and Suffering," 346-49; Bell, *Liberation Theology,* 146-53.

22. Bell, *Liberation Theology,* 70-74, 149-51.

23. Ibid., 189-95.

24. Richard J. Mouw, "Violence and the Atonement," in *Must Christianity Be Violent?*

Reflections on History, Practice, and Theology, ed. Kenneth R. Chase and Alan Jacobs (Grand Rapids, MI: Brazos Press, 2003), 159-71.

25. For versions of this argument, see William C. Placher, "Christ Takes Our Place: Rethinking Atonement," *Interpretation* 53, no. 1 (January 1999): 16-17; Thelma Megill-Cobbler, "A Feminist Rethinking of Punishment Imagery in Atonement," *Dialog* 35, no. 1 (Winter 1996): 19-20; Leanne Van Dyk, "Do Theories of Atonement Foster Abuse?" *Dialog* 35, no.1 (Winter 1996): 24; Houts, "Atonement and Abuse," 29.

26. Thanks to Leann Van Dyk, who suggested this particular name for the motif that I was developing.

27. For a detailed discussion of the seven seals, see Weaver, *The Nonviolent Atonement,* 20-28.

28. M. Eugene Boring, *Revelation,* Interpretation: A Bible Commentary for Teaching and Preaching (Louisville: John Knox Press, 1989), 130-31.

29 Walter Wink, *Engaging the Powers: Discernment and Resistance in a World of Domination,* vol. 3, *The Powers* (Minneapolis: Fortress Press, 1992), 175-84.

30. Two reasons make it important to underscore our participation in the forces of evil that killed Jesus. Theologically, it asserts universal sinfulness as well as stating the link that enables us to share in the victory of Jesus' resurrection over those powers of evil. Historically, it is important to lay responsibility for resistance to the reign of God and the death of Jesus on all of humanity, beginning with the Roman political establishment that had the final human responsibility, as a counter to the claim that "the Jews" killed Jesus, which became the basis of anti-Semitism through the centuries since Constantine. See Carroll, *Constantine's Sword,* 71-88, 175-76.

31. David G. Hunter, "The Christian Church and the Roman Army in the First Three Centuries," in *The Church's Peace Witness,* ed. Marlin E. Miller and Barbara Nelson Gingerich (Grand Rapids, MI: Eerdmans, 1994), 161-81; David G. Hunter, "A Decade of Research on Early Christians and Military Service," *Religious Studies Review* 18, no. 2 (April 1992): 87-94; David M. Scholer, "Early Christian Attitudes to War and Military Service: A Selective Bibliography," *TSF Bulletin* 8, no. 1 (September-October 1984): 23-24.

32. J. Christiaan Beker, *Paul the Apostle: The Triumph of God in Life and Thought* (Philadelphia: Fortress, 1980), 135-212; Raymund Schwager, *Jesus in the Drama of Salvation* (New York: Crossroad, 1999), 160-68.

RESPONSES TO
J. DENNY WEAVER

Response to J. Denny Weaver
Hans Boersma

All three traditional atonement models, argues Weaver, run into trouble because they accept violence. Whether it is the traditional *Christus Victor* model (with "God handing the Son over... as a ransom payment,"[1] or with a "cosmic battle" leading to victory[2]), the Anselmian satisfaction theory (in which God "arranges for Jesus to die to pay the debt to God's honor"[3]), or the Abelardian moral influence theory (where "the Father has one of his children...killed in order to show love to the rest of the Father's children"[4]), they all implicate God in violence. We are duty bound, therefore, according to Weaver, to abandon them all. To be sure, a small ray of light does peek through the darkness of the Christian tradition. Weaver sees some positive elements in the early church's *Christus Victor* theme, as it operated on the basis of the church being pacifist and distinct from the wider social order.[5]

Not only does Weaver argue that we should reject all traditional models for their collusion with violence, but he also claims to have produced the one theory that avoids and answers "all the errors and problems" inherent in these traditional atonement images.[6] I cannot help but approach such a rather grand claim with a degree of skepticism. The sharp and unequivocal manner in which the tradition is discarded only adds to my skepticism. Are we to assume that the entire Christian tradition has failed in its appropriation of the biblical witness? The traditional theory of divine *concursus*—according to which divine and human agents are simultaneously involved in a particular action—is dismissed out of hand as "nonsense," as it "renders meaningless any attempt to use theology to express Christian faith."[7] Classic atonement doctrine becomes "child abuse" as the Father "arranges the death of one child for the benefit of the others."[8] Those trying to avoid this charge by introducing trinitarian theology and by speaking of the Father as suffering with the Son are chastised for the notion of "the Father engaging in self-abuse—which might be called divine suicide."[9] The reader is left to choose: either the entire Christian tradition has gone disastrously wrong in assuming that God has a purpose with the cross or there is something wrong with Weaver's argument.

I believe the latter to be the case, and let me come clean right away by saying that I believe that tradition has normative value. One of the distinguishing marks of the Anabaptist movement is its unequivocal rejection of the value of tradition. It is my conviction that throughout history God's Spirit has led the church to discern the apostolic truth, so that there can never be an unequivocal clear-cut disconnect between earlier and later periods in the history of Christian doctrine. Underlying much of the discussion we're having in this book is a difference in approach to authority. Are we entitled to interpret the Scriptures on our own, or do we read within the boundaries of the apostolic tradition and creedal affirmations?[10] My view is that theology ought to do the latter. But even if we hold to a more radical notion of *sola scriptura*, shouldn't we still expect some degree of continuity between earlier and later stages in the interpretation of Scripture? In other words, if one needs to discard the entire tradition with its various atonement theologies in order to establish one's own, the plausibility of the resulting new theory can hardly be rated high.

Weaver laments the acceptance of divine violence within the traditional atonement theories as part of their explanation of the cross. But it is not clear to me why nonviolence figures so prominently in his approach, since by his own definition, Weaver clearly accepts the need for violence. He defines it as "harm or damage."[11] Since I have already critiqued Weaver's understanding of violence in my own chapter, I will be brief here. Few people truly believe that any and all infliction of "harm or damage" is immoral. Indeed, in his book *Nonviolent Atonement*, Weaver makes quite clear that he believes inflicting "harm or damage" can be a good thing. The coercion that he advocates includes social ostracism, economic boycotts, punishing children, knocking a person out of the path of a vehicle, and physically restraining a person attempting suicide.[12] Presumably, Weaver would justify the harm done in these situations by appealing to the greater benefits that these actions also produce. If violence simply means any "harm or damage," it is hard to see how anyone could be a consistent defender of nonviolence. Clearly, Weaver accepts violence by his own definition. I do not believe that this acceptance is a negative thing. Weaver's case illustrates that almost all of us operate on the basis that inflicting some harm or damage, whether physical or otherwise, is not only acceptable but may, at times, be a good thing.

But apart from definitional matters, there is something theologically deeply unsettling about the impression Weaver gives of an abusive God who punishes his child as an innocent third party. Throughout his essay, Weaver juxtaposes "God" and "Jesus." He comments, for instance, "Some scholars have attempted to blunt the fact that God needed and orchestrated the death of Jesus by arguing that Jesus submitted voluntarily to the death that would satisfy God's honor or God's law."[13] And Weaver depicts what happens according to substitutionary atonement as follows: "God punishes— abuses—one of God's children for the sake of the others. And the Jesus of this motif models passive submission to innocent and unjust suffering for the sake of others."[14] These comments make one curious about Weaver's underlying Christology. His *Nonviolent Atonement* makes clear that he has grave difficulties with the traditional Chalcedonian understanding of Jesus as both divine and human.[15] But if Jesus is truly one with the Father—of the same substance with the Father—then what happens on the cross is not a transaction between *two individuals,* one of whom is abusing the other! It is only because Weaver has abandoned orthodox Christology that he now has difficulty seeing the justice of a penal view of atonement.

It also makes quite a difference *how* one understands penal substitution. Weaver decries the assumption "that doing justice means to punish," an image that "assumes the necessity of punishment, with innocent Jesus punished in our place."[16] The question is: Does justice always exclude punishment? It is quite possible, of course, to be so driven by the desire for revenge that justice—the restoration of relationships— becomes entirely impossible. But such blind craving for revenge does not imply that all punishment is wrong. Indeed, our society would become much less just if we removed all punishment. Opposition to any and all punishment only encourages the endemic abuse of innocent victims! Of course, if Jesus is an innocent third party punished in our place, this would be problematic. But it seems to me that this critique of traditional atonement theory is based on a caricature. Traditional atonement theology, in line with Irenaeus, looks to the incarnation, and to Jesus' life, death, and resurrection, as recapitulation: Jesus retraces and so heals all of human life. Jesus is not a third party punished in our place but rather is himself the new Israel and the new Adam—the one who in his own Person includes all Israel and all humanity. A more careful engagement of the tradition than we find in Weaver would enable us to find in this tradition rich resources for our adoration of the love and justice of God in Jesus Christ.

Notes

1. Weaver, 5.
2. Ibid., 2.
3. Ibid., 5.
4. Ibid., 6.
5. Weaver works with what has been called the "Constantinian fall paradigm." (Cf. D. H. Williams, *Retrieving the Tradition and Renewing Evangelicalism: A Primer for Suspicious Protestants* [Grand Rapids, MI: Eerdmans, 1999], 101-31.) This paradigm argues that violence became the acceptable modus operandi for the church after the Christianizing of the Roman Empire in the fourth century, which ultimately led to the popularizing of the violent satisfaction theories of atonement in Anselm and later Reformed theology. I am a little puzzled at Weaver's comment that with the "Constantinian synthesis" the "narrative *Christus Victor* could fade away." In *The Nonviolent Atonement* (Grand Rapids, MI: Eerdmans, 2001), 14-15, 70-98, Weaver sharply distinguishes the "classical" *Christus Victor* theme (which employed violence) from his own (nonviolent) "narrative" *Christus Victor* theme.
6. Weaver's claim—stated no less than three times in his essay—focuses in particular on satisfaction accounts of atonement, but he clearly has in mind all traditional theories.
7. Weaver, 6.
8. Ibid., 7.
9. Ibid., 16.
10. Thomas Finger is the only one who in his essay explicitly mentions this issue when he insists that "the Bible will provide the main source and sole norm of the theology below." Due to his appropriation of elements from the early church and from Eastern Orthodoxy, however, Finger tends to remain far more solidly within the orbit of traditional atonement theology than does Weaver.
11. Weaver, 2.
12. Weaver, *Nonviolent Atonement*, 9.
13. Weaver, 5.
14. Ibid., 8.
15. Weaver, *Nonviolent Atonement*, 92-96.
16. Weaver, 7-8.

Response to J. Denny Weaver
Thomas Finger

Weaver sharpens an issue that runs through all four essays in this volume. This issue is: how often, and exactly where, must theologians pronounce "either/or" affirmations; and how often and where can they make "both/and" statements? Either/or affirmations draw sharp lines between that which must be asserted to express the Christian faith, and the opposite, which must be rejected. "There is a God" over against "There is no God" is a simple example. Both/and statements combine affirmations that may seem contradictory, but which, a theologian claims, are compatible (such as "God is one" and "God is three").

Weaver, in opposition to Boersma, and more explicitly than Daniels, treats substitutionary (or satisfaction or penal) atonement in either/or fashion. He insists that "It should be abandoned,"[1] but that his narrative *Christus Victor* model "avoids all the problematic elements in classic atonement images."[2] In this way, Weaver underlines a major issue emerging from these essays: Must substitutionary atonement as a whole be rejected because it allegedly sanctions violence that is incompatible with Christian faith?

Like Weaver, I affirm, as either/or, that Christian theology must conceive God's atoning work as nonviolent—as excluding direct, divine exercise of violence. Yet I find some value in the substitutionary model. Our two essays, then, and indirectly the other two, raise the question: To reject divine violence in either/or fashion, must substitution be rejected in the same either/or manner? Because of this question's importance in all four essays, I will form my response to Weaver around it, even though I find other issues more attractive.

I fully share Weaver's concern that today's church must "maintain itself as distinct from the prevailing social order."[3] This also is an either/or issue for me. Any group that calls itself a church but assimilates to its society in every important way cannot be a church of Jesus Christ. I also seek to challenge "the extent to which presuppositions of violence as well as overt violence are intrinsic to supposed standard Christian theology," and also theology's failures "to challenge violence" as well as its "actual accommodation of violence and injustice."[4]

Like Weaver, I favor *Christus Victor,* although his "narrative" version seems to operate mostly on the historical plane, or in what I call this model's *conflictive dimension,* and much less on a plane involving transcendent powers, or its *transformative dimension.* Nevertheless, Weaver stresses Jesus' resurrection, and acknowledges the *transformative dimension* when he insists that participation in God's reign is possible only through grace, because "we cannot resist and overcome the powers of evil" by our own power. "Only God can do that, and if we are resisting and overcoming, it is because God enables it."[5]

Weaver, like me, draws biblical support from the Gospels. But his strong reliance on Revelation surprises me. I agree that "the victory of the reign of God over the evil symbolized by Rome occurs *nonviolently*" in this book.[6] Nevertheless, no New Testament writing portrays God as the apparent author of violent destruction so often. If Weaver is to make consistent sense of this apocalypse, and of multiple other biblical texts that present God similarly, it seems that he cannot simply deny "that violence is divinely willed,"[7] but must ask in precisely what sense God might make use of it.

To dialogue further, I must carefully contrast my approach with the one that Weaver, to the best of my understanding, seems to take. I endeavor to start from biblical narrative, and then craft concepts appropriate to what I find there. No one, of course, approaches the Bible without presuppositions, and mine will shape what I read. Nevertheless, it is quite possible, and desirable, to keep working toward greater convergence between one's own concepts and Scripture as a (not fully attainable) goal.

I try not to assume that God could or could not employ violence, but to discover how divine judgment actually operates. I find that God frequently judges sinners by abandoning them, or handing them over, to the gods they choose. I also notice, surprisingly, that Scripture very often ascribes these acts not only to God, but also to those death-dealing forces. For example, Yahweh is frequently said to judge Judah by sending her into Babylonian exile. But this same judgment is also ascribed quite often to the Babylonians.

This judgment, accordingly, must be called God's judgment on Judah's injustice, unfaithfulness, and idolatry. Yet God is only the remote, or indirect, cause of the actual events involved. The active, direct cause is the Babylonian army. Since this pattern appears very frequently in Scripture, I conceptualize it by distinguishing *indirect* from *direct* judgment—and consequently, indirect from direct use of violence. I propose that theology can attribute the former to God (contra Weaver), but not the latter (contra Boersma).

Systematically speaking, Weaver appears to start mainly with assumptions about violence and nonviolence and the apparent logical structure of atonement theories. He notices that if the judgment language just described were applied to the cross, it would mean "that both Jesus and those who kill Jesus would be carrying out the will of God." But Weaver calls this "nonsense," for these appear to him "mutually exclusive" categories. They can be combined only by "cloaking them" in an unintelligible "category such as mystery."[8] But how can anyone know which categories are "mutually exclusive" in biblical narrative, except by examining it?

Such an examination, I propose, shows that such judgment language is neither murky mystery nor flat contradiction. It is paradox, or apparent contradiction, which is required to describe judgment's historical operation. Theology can unravel it to a significant extent.

Further, I employ theological atonement motifs not, as Weaver supposes, to "salvage . . . and integrate them" all,[9] but as lenses to help me spot major biblical themes. Weaver insists that these motifs are "separate and distinct approaches."[10] Yet I find that they frequently overlap in theology's actual history. Substitutionary motifs often function more metaphorically than they do in Weaver's strict propositional interpretation.

When I mention substitution favorably, I mean that this "lens" helps me discover biblical passages that represent Jesus doing "something *for us*, and also *before* us and *outside* of us, which he gives *to us*."[11] This model points to texts that represent what Jesus did and what we receive as some sort of exchange, occurring according to some pattern beyond our subjective experience.[12] Since substitution furnishes some concepts for this, I give it credit. If Weaver wishes to discredit this model entirely, he must address these passages and provide a superior conceptualization.

This overall pattern might, metaphorically, be called a "law." But having discovered it with some help from the substitutionary model, I hardly need to call it one that God "needs," or of which God is a "target." From other biblical texts I learn that it resulted from the creation of beings that could freely turn toward God, the source of all life. If they do, they begin participating in eternal life. But if they turn away from eternal life, they turn, by definition, toward eternal death. God, who created them freely, hardly "needs" this pattern in some anthropomorphic sense. It is simply how a universe containing free creatures functions.

To be sure, God willed this pattern, and allowed for those tragedies that result from choices for death. This overall operation of justice must be ascribed in some sense to God. Yet it is nonviolent, for "violence is coercive and deprives its victims of freedom. But this justice respects our freedom and lets us follow the course we choose."[13]

However, if atonement models are "separate and distinct,"[14] as Weaver declares at the outset, one model cannot occasionally overlap or supplement another (both/and). We must choose either *Christus Victor* or substitution. If (narrative) *Christus Victor* is entirely correct, substitution must be entirely incorrect. Diverse atonement models cannot function as lenses to help us appropriate different biblical emphases. They must, apparently, be distinct logical structures and be evaluated, as correct or incorrect, on that level.

Substitution, as Weaver defines it, always includes, among others, the propositions that: "doing justice or righting wrongs depends on retribution";[15] God's "modus operandi is retributive violence";[16] Jesus images "passive, innocent submission to abuse and oppression";[17] and God therefore appears as a "divine avenger or punisher and/or as a child abuser."[18] If what one means by "substitution" must include these propositions, I would reject it too.

I suspect that substitutionary theories need not affirm all these assertions—even though this model, indeed, is sometimes used to endorse them. But I leave that matter to its proponents. My point is simply that some substitutionary notions that reflect important biblical themes make sense within a conceptualization of biblical narrative that rejects Weaver's four propositions. I merely propose that substitution, as I use the term, can sometimes contribute to such a conceptualization, and need not be rejected entirely to affirm nonviolent atonement.

Once again, I do affirm, as either/or, that Christian theology must conceive God's atoning work as nonviolent, or as excluding direct divine exercise of violence (contra Boersma). I also assert, as either/or, that authentic churches will be distinct from their societies, not assimilated to them in every important respect (pro Weaver and Daniels). But I find it incorrect, theologically, to link these two either/ors inseparably to a third, between substitution and a correct atonement theory. Practically, I doubt whether those who insist on this link will have great success in efforts to persuade audiences strongly influenced by substitution.

Notes

1. Weaver, 2.
2. Ibid., 24.
3. Ibid., 23.
4. Ibid., 26.
5. Ibid., 22.
6. Ibid., 19.
7. Ibid., 1.
8. Ibid., 6.
9. Ibid., 1.
10. Ibid., 2.
11. Finger, 105.
12. Among the many are Matthew 20:28; Mark 10:45; John 10:15; Romans 4:25, 5:6-10; 1 Corinthians 1:30; 2 Corinthians 5:14-15, 21; Colossians 1:22; 1 Timothy 2:2; Hebrews 9:12, 10:12-14; 1 Peter 1:18-19, 2:24; 1 John 4:10; Revelation 1:6. I am not suggesting that all these are best interpreted in a substitutionary sense, but only that it is often helpful to consider these and others through the substitutionary "lens."
13. Finger, 98.
14. Weaver, 2.
15. Ibid., 7.
16. Ibid., 16.
17. Ibid.
18. Ibid., 7.

Response to J. Denny Weaver
T. Scott Daniels

A member of my congregation purchased a large block of tickets to the Ash Wednesday opening of Mel Gibson's *Passion of the Christ* and asked me—as his pastor—to come along so that I could answer any questions of a theological nature that the group might have after viewing the film. I accepted with mixed emotions. I strongly wanted to avoid getting caught in the middle of the passion over *The Passion* from both supporters and detractors, and I frankly was not anxious to witness the highly publicized graphic violence that dominated the film.

I left the film still conflicted. There were many beautiful and well-done moments in the movie and I was very thankful for the kind of dialogue both inside and outside the church that occurred after its theatrical release. In the end, however, my primary criticism of *The Passion of the Christ* was not the graphic violence or the obvious theological interpretations that influenced the script; my concern was that because the film centered exclusively on the crucifixion of Christ—with only a couple of small exceptions—the death of Jesus was completely separated out from the rest of his life and ministry. I realize that a filmmaker can only do so much in a couple of hours, but if one did not know the Gospel narratives well, one could easily watch this powerful demonstration of the crucifixion without understanding any of the factors leading to the cross, and certainly without understanding what it might mean to "take up the cross" as a disciple.[1]

I sense that my concern with Gibson's movie is very similar in nature to J. Denny Weaver's critique of the dominant theories of the atonement in the West—particularly Anselmian theories of substitution. In trying to emphasize "narrative" as part of any theory of atonement, Weaver is trying to keep us from divorcing God's activity in Christ upon the cross from the rest of his life and teaching. If Weaver is correct—which I believe he is—theories of substitution tend to focus exclusively on the cross and view the life of Christ as some kind of moral addition. What Weaver wants instead is for us to have an atonement theory based upon the life and teachings of Jesus. Rather than focusing solely upon the death of

Christ, this narrative *Christus Victor* theory would view the cross as a lens for illuminating and understanding of the way of the kingdom already articulated and embodied in the life of Jesus.

I wholeheartedly agree with Weaver's assessment that the classic theories of atonement in the West have suffered from "the implications of Anselm's own move to delete the devil from the atonement equation, leaving God as the only actor with agency in the equation."[2] He is correct that if we are going to restore or renew atonement theology by removing God as the primary agent of violence, the result will look something akin to a "narrative *Christus Victor*."

Although I am in full agreement with Weaver that we need something besides God's honor or God's law to be the basis of a viable atonement theory, I am not completely unsympathetic to Anselm's desire to delete the devil from the "salvation equation." There is certainly a great deal in the hyperspiritualized popular form of the *Christus Victor* theory of Anselm's day that made it worthy of critique. However, if we were able to expand our understanding of evil—as Weaver tries to do—to encompass not just Satan but the totality of "principalities and powers,"[3] not only would the "activist mission" of the life of Jesus become relevant to the narrative of atonement, but I am convinced that we would become better interpreters of both the Old Testament and Revelation as well.

Weaver's proposal would move us away from legal frameworks of atonement toward more relational understandings. In the Genesis narratives this would help us understand original sin in relational terms such as shame, blame, and rejection rather than their legal counterparts. We could then interpret Cain's sin as a violation of brotherly relatedness rather than a trespass against the divine law. In the Noah narratives it would make sense to us that God is grieved not because his honor has been violated, but because the world was corrupt; it was "filled with violence" (Gen. 6:11). Even the last of the pre-Abrahamic narratives—Babel—could be interpreted not as a violation against divine decree but as the broken consequences of the pride of powers that divide culture against culture and nation against nation.

A narrative *Christus Victor* could help make sense of the narrative function that the possessors of the land—such as the Egyptians, the Canaanites, or the Babylonians—have in Israel's struggle to be the unique people of God. The Old Testament interprets Israel's struggle as a battle against these "powers" rather than as a laboring to regain God's honor or justify God's laws. The frequent Exodus references in the birth narratives of Luke, for example, make much more sense if we understand Jesus as a new Moses who is coming to "bring good news to the poor . . . to proclaim release to the captives and recovery of sight to the blind, to let the oppressed go free, to proclaim the year of the Lord's favor" (Luke 4:18-19) than if we view his coming as the fulfillment of divine retributive justice.

One question I have for Weaver is, although I understand why he favors the *Christus Victor* theory over the moral influence theory, wouldn't putting the principalities and powers back as the object of the atonement also help redeem Moral Influence as a workable theory? I found his historical description of the development of the three classic theories very helpful; but I wonder if the narrative *Christus Victor* theory would benefit from at least a hint of the moral influence theory in terms of a description of how the love of God—which is the source of divine victory—shapes not only Christ's mission but also the mission of his disciples. Weaver's theory may not need such influence because he certainly understands that it is the mission of Christ to overcome evil with good. However, I believe it is essential in removing God as the primary actor in the atonement that we emphasize the ongoing nature of Christ's victory as it continues through those who participate in the kingdom of God.

Again the Old Testament gives us a trajectory for understanding this narratively. As scholars such as John Howard Yoder have pointed out, we must never forget the strange and even silly battles that take place prior to Israel's decision to become just like all the other nations. For example, in Judges chapter 7, Gideon starts with 30,000 soldiers and ends up with 300 men who "drink like dogs." Yet this is the very "army" that leads to victory when the violence of the enemy is turned in upon itself.

The struggle for Israel—until 1 Samuel 8—is whether they are going to be a nation that has Yahweh as their king, a nation that does not trust in chariots, horses, and swords, or whether they are going to become like all the other nations and have all of the trappings of power that come with a king. After they receive the consequences of being just another nation, the prophets begin to call them back to justice and to mercy. The call upon their life is to beat swords into plowshares and spears into pruning hooks. Israel is to live toward the ideal of the Holy Mountain of Isaiah 11, where lion and lamb lay down together without destroying each other.

Therefore, I would argue that in the narrative *Christus Victor* theory, the cross is not just illuminated by the life and teaching of Jesus, but it is also clarified by the entire activity of God with his people in the Old Testament.

The point that I am trying to make is that one of the additional problems with the substitutionary framework is that it has to wrestle with the question of God's timing. If God is not only the primary agent in the atonement, but also the one in need of the action or results of the death of Christ, why wait so long to enact the atonement? Why not fulfill the requirements of divine justice immediately rather than leave generations of people lost under the requirements of the law?

The best answer that the theory of substitution could give is that we cannot presume to know the mind and will of God, and we must trust that Christ came in "the fullness of time."

The obvious benefit of a narrative *Christus Victor* is that it makes the life, death, and resurrection of Christ completely consistent with the activity of God already taking place in his self-revelation to Israel. Although the incarnation is certainly new and radically different than God's work with Israel, the core activity of God in Christ is essentially old—revealing what it means to be a people who participate in the kingdom of God, delivering people from the oppressive principalities, and overcoming the violence and evil of the powers with love and good.

I cannot help but think that Weaver's suggestions could also help us read Revelation in better ways than we often do. In the fifth chapter of Revelation John gets to glimpse the throne room of heaven—he gets access to the control room of the universe. There he finds the heavenly congregation surrounding the scroll of history sealed with its seven seals. No one in heaven or on earth or under the earth is found worthy to unroll the scroll and control the trajectory of history. John weeps bitterly until one of the elders tells him, "Do not weep. See, the Lion of the tribe of Judah, the Root of David, has conquered, so that he can open the scroll and its seven seals" (v. 5).

The image is so clear. The one who finally embodied the continual Word and activity of God has conquered all principalities and powers—*Christus est Dominus.* Yet, the most important image occurs in the next verse: "I saw between the throne and the four living creatures and among the elders a Lamb standing as if it had been slaughtered" (v. 6). The most amazing image of Revelation and the key to the narrative *Christus Victor* theory of the atonement is that the Lion is the Lamb. The principalities and powers—embodied in the image of Babylon—are finally overcome by the self-giving love of the Lamb.

I preached a sermon not long ago on the amazing revelation that the Lion is the Lamb—the powerful one is found in the image of vulnerability. Afterward, a dear lady came to me and said, "I liked your sermon, but I still think the Lion who is the Lamb will become the Lion again."

What J. Denny Weaver helps us see in articulating a narrative *Christus Victor* is that too often in our substitutionary theories of atonement in which "violence is divinely willed" we make the Lamb the Lion. Instead, what we need to understand is that the one who confronted the forces of evil with good calls each of us who are horribly marked by the powers of the beast to participate in a cruciform life that not only overcomes the forces of evil with good, but marks our life with the Lamb until we become the city that "has no need of sun or moon to shine on it, for the glory of God is its light, and its lamp is the Lamb" (Rev. 21:23).

Notes

1. I believe this is part of the reason the claims by some that the film is anti-Semitic have some credibility. If there is no context present that describes why the life and teachings of Christ were offensive to all principalities and powers, one could easily be left with the conclusion that—despite the fact that Jesus and the other disciples were Jewish—the Jewish leaders simply hated Jesus and manipulated the political situation in order to have him killed.

2. Weaver, 7.

3. I am thinking here of the work of Walter Wink in particular.

CHAPTER 2

VIOLENCE, THE CROSS, AND DIVINE INTENTIONALITY: A MODIFIED REFORMED VIEW

Hans Boersma

At the heart of the debate on the link between violence and the atonement lies the question of divine intentionality. Is the cross part of God's plan of redemption? Put differently, does Jesus' willingness to suffer for the world imply conformity to the will of God? Or is the cross merely the result of the evil plotting of human beings? Is the cross an instance of human *and* divine violence, or is it an instance only of human violence? And if, along with the broad Christian tradition we make a dual affirmation, what does this mean for our theology and for our interpersonal relationships? The idea that God might be involved in violence, precisely in the manifestation of his love on the cross, leads to questions about the nature of God, which we dare not avoid. Traditional atonement models, comments Rita Nakashima Brock, reflect "images of the neglect of children or, even worse, child abuse, making it acceptable as divine behavior—cosmic child abuse, as it were."[1] The idea of the Father sending his Son as an innocent third party to the cross raises questions about the character of the God we worship. What is more, if we worship a violent God this has implications for human actions. If violence is justified for God, isn't it justified also for humans? According to many, there is a fairly direct link between divine child abuse and human child abuse, especially since the biblical account intimates that we are made in the image of God. And while traditional atonement theories seem to encourage human *perpetrators* of violence, these theories also appear to say to the *victims* that they had better accept their lot in life. Traditional theories seem to intimate that one's willingness to suffer—self-sacrifice—is a good thing. Darby Kathleen Ray objects to this, commenting that "the salvific values of suffering, self-sacrifice, and obedience are too easily distorted into a theological tool of subjugation."[2]

In this essay I will mount a defense of the traditional atonement models by presenting a modified Reformed view that draws on Irenaeus and N. T. Wright. I will argue that God's involvement in the cross is a true embodiment of his love, that the divine violence involved in the cross is a necessary corollary of God's acceptance of the boundaries of the created order, and that the ultimate "theodicy" of divine violence lies in the resurrection as the completion of the Paschal mystery. My argument will proceed as follows: I will (1) indicate where I believe Reformed theories of the atonement have overaccentuated divine violence; (2) outline how traditional atonement theologies have dealt with the violence and atonement issue; (3) briefly outline Irenaeus's recapitulation theory and N. T. Wright's notion of reconstitution; (4) present a defense of the Reformed (or Augustinian) position that punishment and violence are not universally to be rejected; and (5) indicate the importance of this modified Reformed view in upholding the very possibility of community.

Reformed Overaccentuation of Violence

Objections to divine violence extend to each of the traditional accounts of the cross. Reformed views, usually characterized as penal substitutionary in character, are not the only ones that are being criticized. And, as we shall see momentarily, critics are right not to single out substitutionary atonement theology as the only view that faces the problem of having to reconcile divine love and divine violence. All the same, Calvinist accounts of atonement theology are more vulnerable than other views to the objection that they implicate God in violence. Calvinists, after all, have traditionally emphasized double predestination from eternity—a notion that many would interpret as involving God in arbitrariness and unnecessary violence (depending, to be sure, on one's definition of violence). The Reformed understanding of limited atonement, moreover, has tended to restrict the divine intent of the cross to the elect, who alone will ultimately be saved from damnation and enjoy eternal life. Again, the limiting nature of divine redemption on the cross raises questions of divine exclusion and violence. In this essay, I will not deal with questions surrounding predestination and limited atonement.[3] I will only deal with questions arising from the meaning of the atonement itself— does a Reformed position, usually characterized as a penal substitutionary view, obscure the love of God by implicating God in unnecessary or unjustified violence? It seems to me that some of the traditional high Calvinist explanations of the atonement do indeed fall prey to such problems in upholding the love of God. The accusations of juridicizing, individualizing, and dehistoricizing are not entirely without warrant.[4]

Let me briefly explain how some strands of Reformed atonement theology are susceptible to these charges. (I will keep this section brief, trusting that my interlocutors will not disappoint in their critiques of the Reformed tradition.)[5] First, it seems to me that Calvinist covenant theology has tended to view our relationship with God too exclusively through a legal grid. In such views, Christ perfectly fulfilled Adam's legal obligation, both by obeying the law of nature (active obedience) and by suffering the punishment of eternal death on the cross (passive obedience). Where all human beings failed to live up to the demands of God's Law, it was Christ who completely fulfilled them, thereby procuring forgiveness and eternal life for the elect, who would come to believe in Christ. This covenantal framework implied a substitutionary punishment that was thoroughly juridical in character. Moreover, since vicarious substitution meant that Christ took the place of certain (elect) individuals, Christ was seen as bearing the penalty of *my* particular sins that *I* had committed. There is no denying that there is a tendency here toward an economic exchange model of the atonement: my sins are transferred or imputed to Christ while his righteousness is directly transferred or imputed to me. Finally, this scheme minimized the historical link between Christ and Israel. The transaction between Christ and the elect could have taken place at any time and at any place. With the "curse of the Law" referring to the eternal punishment that Christ suffered vicariously for the elect, Calvinist theology obscured the narrative of redemption within which the cross had its place.

The question, of course, is whether such objections—to my mind often overemphasized because of underlying objections not only to high Calvinist theology, but to traditional atonement theories in general— mean that Reformed atonement theology is entirely based on a wrong foundation and that therefore we ought to discard such theology altogether. To my mind, this would be to throw out the baby with the bathwater. I believe that it is quite possible to construct an atonement theology that includes some of the Reformed distinctives—in particular, the notions of representation (or substitution) and of punishment—without falling into the traps of juridicizing, individualizing, and dehistoricizing. What is more, in what follows I will argue that such a position has a proper place within the broad Christian tradition, and that traditional atonement theologies—including my modified Reformed view—do not obscure but rather accentuate the love of God and do a better job of ensuring true redemption (and eschatological enjoyment of the eternal love of God) than theories that expunge all divine intentionality from the cross.

Traditional Atonement Theologies and Divine Violence

The early church frequently used the imagery of God stretching out his hands on the cross, thereby extending his love to the world, embracing the entire globe in his love. Cyril of Alexandria, for example, commented around AD 347 that God "stretched out His hands on the Cross, that He might embrace the ends of the world; for this Golgotha is the very centre of the earth."[6] This imagery of God stretching out his hands or his arms has several implications. First, it means that on the cross of Christ we do not simply have to do with a barbaric human act but also witness here the love of God himself as he identifies with human beings in sending his Son to suffer for our sake. Regardless of how we interpret the cross, it cannot possibly simply be the punishment of a third party. The accusations of divine child abuse overlook the mystery of the incarnation. God himself is present in Christ, so that the suffering of Christ is never simply the suffering of a human being.[7] Second, Cyril's comment implies divine intentionality. God knowingly and willingly stretches out his hands on the cross in order to redeem humanity. It is this question of divine intentionality that is the crux of the debate in this book. At one level, we could simply refer to the biblical witness, which hardly leaves in doubt that the cross is in line with God's purposes: "We were reconciled to God through the death of his Son," Paul writes in Romans 5:10 (cf. Col. 1:22).[8] To the elders in Ephesus, he says that God bought the church "with the blood of his own Son" (Acts 20:28; cf. Rom. 3:25; Eph. 1:7). Not only so, but also on two occasions the book of Acts explicitly rejects the either/or scenario that sees the cross either as the result of human scheming or of divine purpose. The first time, Peter addresses the Jewish crowds about Jesus: "This man, who was put into your power by the deliberate intention and foreknowledge of God, you took and had crucified and killed by men outside the Law" (Acts 2:23). The second time, the apostles are praying to God about the plotting of Herod and Pontius Pilate "*together* with the gentile *nations* and the *peoples* of Israel, against your holy servant Jesus whom you *anointed*, to bring about the very thing that you in your strength and your wisdom had predetermined should happen" (Acts 4:27-28). At the very least, these biblical passages suggest that the cross is not an event that is separated from divine intentionality.

But I want to go beyond the biblical text to the history of Christian thought. Each of the three traditional atonement models—*Christus Victor*, moral influence, and penal substitution—interpret the cross as the result also of divine intentionality. The *Christus Victor* model, for instance, uses military metaphors to describe human redemption or liberation from the power of the evil one. The second-century church father Irenaeus refers to Satan as the "strong man" whom Christ has bound and robbed (Matt. 12:29).[9] In a characteristic passage, Irenaeus comments:

> For as in the beginning he [the apostate angel of God] enticed man to transgress his Maker's law, and thereby got him into his power; yet his power consists in transgression and apostasy, and with these he bound man [to himself]; so again, on the other hand, it was necessary that

through man himself he should, when conquered, be bound with the same chains with which he had bound man, in order that man, being set free, might return to his Lord, leaving to him (Satan) those bonds by which he himself had been fettered, that is, sin. For when Satan is bound, man is set free; since "none can enter a strong man's house and spoil his goods, unless he first bind the strong man himself."[10]

Irenaeus sees Adam's transgression as "bonds" or "chains" that Satan uses to bind human beings.[11] God in turn puts Satan in chains. Christ "robs" the strong man (Matt. 12:29), "crushes" the devil (Gen. 3:15),[12] and "destroys" death.

Two centuries later, Gregory of Nyssa uses his well-known fishhook analogy to describe how God used fraud or deception in obtaining the redemption of his people:

[I]n order to secure that the ransom in our behalf might be easily accepted by him who required it, the Deity was hidden under the veil of our nature, that so, as with ravenous fish, the hook of the Deity might be gulped down along with the bait of flesh, and thus, life being intro-duced into the house of death, and light shining in darkness, that which is diametrically opposed to light and life might vanish; for it is not in the nature of darkness to remain when light is present, or of death to exist when life is active.[13]

Gregory does not hesitate to speak of this divine activity as a form of deception: "[God] Who is at once the just, and good, and wise one, used His device, in which there was deception, for the salvation of him who had perished, and thus not only conferred benefit on the lost one, but on him, too, who had wrought our ruin."[14] Gregory justifies this divine deception (and, I would add, he could in similar fashion have justified divine violence) by referring to the universal benefit of salvation (*apokatastasis pantōn*): When everyone, even "the introducer of evil him-self," will be freed, the deception will be shown for what it truly is: supreme wisdom.[15] It seems clear to me that the way in which Irenaeus and Gregory employ the *Christus Victor* theme makes it difficult to escape the logic of divine violence. Indeed, the most common criticism of the deception theory is that it appears to implicate God in immorality. Many are convinced that divine deception—like divine violence—compromises God's justice. By using deception, God would employ the same means that Satan had initially used to introduce sin into the world.

It could be that I am stretching the military metaphor too far, and that when we look at the actual "battle" (i.e., the means used to attain victory), we end up with a nonviolent redemption, after all.[16] For example, Irenaeus (unlike Gregory) speaks not of divine deception as constituting the battle, but instead refers to "persuasion." This of course brings us into the realm of the moral influence (or Abelardian) theory, in which it is Christ's teaching or example that brings redemption. Also here, however, it is difficult to escape divine violence altogether. First, in moral influence theories we are still connecting the cross to divine intentionality: the Father sends his Son to die in order to evoke a human response of love.[17] Second, it is not at all evident to me that persuasion is nonviolent. Persuasion has to do with boundaries and the changing of boundary markers. Such boundary skirmishes may well be acts of love (ideally, of course, persuasion is meant for the good of the other), but that does not make them nonviolent.[18] Finally, moral influence theories involve the willingness of the Son to suffer for the sake of others, and, as we have already seen, it is precisely the valorization of suffering (and hence the justification of violence) to which some contemporary scholars object. Moral influence theories may seem to be the most innocuous of the three, but they hardly avoid the problem of divine violence.

I do not need to say a great deal about the third main traditional type of theory, the Anselmian understanding. Whether we simply take Anselm's own understanding of the cross as satisfaction of divine honor, or whether we look to later Reformed views that regard the cross as involving penal substitution and as satisfaction of divine justice, the element of divine intentionality is obvious. The Calvinist view, with its notion of punishment, is perhaps more explicit than any of the other theories that God does associate himself with violence and that divine judicial punishment does have a place in our understanding of the cross.

Contemporary attempts to establish a nonviolent understanding of the cross (i.e., a view that excludes *divine* violence) thus face two hurdles. First, they need to come to grips with the biblical witness that repeatedly associates God with violence, including violence on the cross.[19] Second, they need to face up to the fact that they are out of step with the broad Christian tradition. Unfortunately, for some this does not seem to matter a great deal.

Rita Nakashima Brock and Rebecca Ann Parker, in their recent biograph-ically shaped dialogue with atonement theology, steadfastly refuse to acknowledge any involvement of God in the cross. Comments Brock, "To say that Jesus' executioners did what was historically necessary for salvation is to say that state terrorism is a good thing, that torture and murder are the will of God."[20] And J. Denny Weaver discounts not only a penal view of the atonement but also the moral theory, because here "God the Father sent his most precious possession to die in order to display an ultimately loving act. Apparently the death of Jesus has no salvific purpose in this motif if it is not God-intended."[21] Weaver deliberately sets up his interpre-tation of the cross in direct opposition to the violence that he observes in each of the main theories of the Christian tradition.[22] A nonviolent atone-ment may not be problematic for those to whom tradition is nothing but extra ballast that we could just as well do without. But those who believe that their convictions ought to be in continuity with the history of the apostolic tradition will think twice before eliminating from the cross any notion of divine intentionality and divine violence.

Atonement as Recapitulation and Reconstitution

A modified Reformed view of the atonement is able to incorporate each of the three traditional atonement theories. It seems to me that Irenaeus's notion of the recapitulation of Adam and N. T. Wright's under-standing of the reconstitution of Israel are particularly helpful in this regard. The notions of recapitulation and reconstitution can function as the paradigmatic framework within which each of the traditional models has its place.

The term *recapitulation* stems from the Letter to the Ephesians, which explains that God "would bring everything together under Christ, as head, everything in the heavens and everything on earth" (Eph. 1:10)—though Irenaeus works out this notion in far more detail than does the Pauline Letter.[23] The idea of bringing all of creation together under Christ as head—the word *recapitulation* stems from the Latin *caput*, mean-ing "head"—turns out to be a fruitful theme for Irenaeus's understanding of the atonement. The theme of recapitulation is a way of expressing the idea of representation or reconstitution. For Irenaeus, Christ represents all of Adamic humanity. As humanity's representative, he takes their position.[24] Since Christ comes to us as the second Adam, the incarnation of the Word and the life of Christ are important elements in Irenaeus's thought. The incarnation is part of Christ's recapitulation: just as Adam was molded from untilled virgin soil (Gen. 2:5), so Christ was born of a virgin.[25] And it is in the obedience of his life, rejecting the temptations of the devil, that Christ nullifies Adam's disobedience.[26] But recapitulation also includes Christ's death on the cross: the record of our debt has been fastened to the cross for the remission of sins, "so that as by means of a tree we were made debtors to God, [so also] by means of a tree we may obtain the remission of our debt."[27]

For Irenaeus, Christ's work of recapitulation involves every moment of Christ's life, from the time of his incarnation to his death on the cross. This broad scope enables him also to incorporate elements that later theologians often came to regard as mutually exclusive. Irenaeus's notion of recapitulation allows him to look to Christ's work as involving a battling of the devil (*Christus Victor*), a modelling of obedience and a teaching (persuasion) of true knowledge (moral influence), and—to some extent—even a propitiating of the wrath of God. One of the exciting elements in the notion of recapitulation is that it coheres well with all three traditional models. The reason for this is that recapitulation itself is a formal rather than a material concept. When we say that Christ recapitulated Israel and Adam, we have not yet said *in which way* Christ recapitulated them. This is where the three atonement models come in. It is as the representative of Israel and Adam that Christ instructs us and models for us the love of God (moral influence). It is as the representative of Israel and Adam that Christ suffers God's judgement on evil and bears the suffering of the curse of the Law (penal representation). It is as the representative of Israel and Adam that Christ fights the powers of evil, expels demons, withstands satanic temptation to the point of death, and rises victorious from the grave (*Christus Victor*). One of the most intriguing elements of Irenaeus's atonement theology is his ability to combine the various atonement models by means of his understanding of recapitulation.[28]

N. T. Wright's understanding of Christ's redemptive work as the reconstitution of Israel is particularly helpful for an appreciation of the much maligned role of punishment in the work of redemption.[29] As we have already seen, traditional Reformed theology referred Paul's "curse of the Law" (Gal. 3:10) to the eternal punishment deserved by all who, like Adam, failed to observe even the most minute detail of the Law.[30] If, however, Jesus' role is to retrace Israel's history and so to reconstitute the nation, perhaps this means that we need to look to the historic failures of Israel to find out the meaning of the "curse of the Law." When in Galatians 3:10 Paul makes reference to Deuteronomy 27:26, he has in mind the historical and corporate context of Deuteronomy.[31] The Deuteronomic curse of the Law, although broad ranging, ultimately has reference to Babylonian exile.[32] The Paschal mystery of the cross and the resurrection, then, is a recapitulation of Israel's exilic punishment and return from exile. As Israel's representative, Christ thus reconstitutes and restores—at least in principle—both Israel and (through Israel) all of Adamic existence.

The Paschal mystery as a reenactment of Israel's exile and restoration implies that divine punishment (and thus divine violence) has a place within the overall scheme of redemption. What we have, essentially, is a modified Reformed position. Whereas the juridical aspect continues to hold an important place, the penal aspect needs to be complemented by moral influence and *Christus Victor* elements. Although individuals certainly benefit from Christ's work, there is no direct transfer or imputation that takes place between Christ and the elect individual. Instead, Christ suffers the corporate curse of Israel and in rising from the dead reconstitutes the people of God. And although Christ's work does result in a new humanity, it does so by means of the historical connection between Israel and Christ as her messianic representative. My understanding of penal representation, therefore, avoids the objections of juridicizing, individualizing, and dehistoricizing that have been levelled against Reformed atonement theology.

The Positive Use of Punishment and Violence

But doesn't the Reformed view, by introducing the notion of punishment, render a problematic understanding of God? Granted that my view is a *modified* Reformed view, doesn't it still labor under the objection that it makes God a violent God and that, by implication, this results in human violence? The assumption behind these questions is, of course, that violence is universally reprehensible. I am not at all convinced that this is the case. If we define violence as any use of force or coercion that involves some kind of hurt or injury—whether this coercion be physical or nonphysical, personal or institutional, incidental or structural—it seems clear that most people are willing to employ some kind of violence. Mandatory vaccination against smallpox is a form of physical coercion to which few would object.[33] We all condone (or rather encourage) a mother stopping her child from crossing the street when to cross would be unsafe. Most of us realize that to never punish a child would also not be in the child's interest. Many, if not most, people are willing to employ economic boycotts to force nations to comply with important legitimate concerns of the international community. In short, we all accept that under certain circumstances it is praiseworthy to inflict harm or injury (to use violence) for the sake of the greater good.

Why, then, do some people insist that they hold to a nonviolent stance, and why do they look to Jesus as the ultimate embodiment of non-violence? Quite often, it seems to me, we simply dub as violent any coercive act that we think is morally reprehensible. Other coercive acts, those that we think are morally acceptable, we refer to as nonviolent. For instance, Weaver opposes racist practices, poverty-dealing social structures, and the criminal justice system because they are violent, whereas he speaks in favor of economic boycotts, knocking a person out of the path of a vehicle, and physically restraining a person attempting to commit suicide, all of which he regards as nonviolent.[34] Clearly, this would imply that one and the same act (e.g., knocking a person or boycotting a nation) could either be violent or nonviolent, depending on whether the action is morally acceptable or not. But what that really means is that Weaver is not as nonviolent as he would like us to believe. He simply refuses to call "violent" those coercive acts with which he happens to find himself in agreement. Presumably, under such a definition, one might even engage in a nonviolent war.

Sure, the suggestion of a nonviolent war is a bit of a tease, and I suspect that Weaver would reject the coercion and harm of any war, and would consider all such coercion violent and as such morally reprehensible. But the tease does have a serious undertone. Let me illustrate my underlying point from Walter Wink's *Engaging the Powers*, a book on which Weaver relies a great deal. Here Wink tries to establish a third way between just war theories associated with Augustine and a radical pacifism or nonresistance that rejects all use of force or coercion. The cycle of revenge, argues Wink, is inherent in the use of violence: "[Violence] inculcates the longing for revenge, and for what the losers call 'justice.' And they will have learned from our example how to use violence more efficiently. *Violence can never stop violence because its very success leads others to imitate it.*"[35] Wink opposes all use of what he terms "redemptive violence." He does not believe, however, that this rejection of violence leaves us without any means of opposing evil. He argues that Jesus' "third way" beyond just war and pacifism is not

> averse to using coercion. His way aims at converting the opponent; failing that, it hopes for accommodation, where the opponent is willing to make some changes simply to get the protesters off his back. But if that too fails, nonviolence entails coercion: the opponent is forced to make a change rather than suffer the loss of power, even though he remains hostile. But Jesus' way does not employ *violent* coercion.[36]

Wink's nonviolent coercion takes on a rather militaristic tone when he not only speaks of "coercion" as a legitimate part of Jesus' "third way," but when he refers to this coercion as a "militant nonviolence" and as a "highly aggressive" nonviolence.[37] Despite his opposition to the Augustinian just war theory, Wink even wishes success to those who in desperation resort to counterviolence.[38]

For the sake of our discussion, however, let us abandon for a moment Weaver's understanding and adopt what I think is the more common view of violence as any coercion that involves some kind of hurt or injury, whether morally acceptable or not. Can divine punishment (clearly a form of violence) be morally acceptable? The question facing Reformed theology here is: Why doesn't God simply forgive? Why does he send his people into exile, and why does Christ recapitulate and reconstitute the life, death, and resurrection of Israel? Why should Christ suffer the exilic curse? As is well known, punishments can serve different goals: prevention, rehabilitation, deterrence, retribution, or some combination of these four.

The first three purposes of punishment in some way or other have the effect of protecting society. Even though the rehabilitative purpose is primarily focused on the cure of the criminal, it also indirectly benefits society since, if the criminal is truly cured, society will not be attacked again. The retributive purpose of punishment is aimed at something greater than society, justice itself, and thus is independent of the good (or, for that matter, the evil) that is brought to others by the execution of the punishment.[39]

Let us assume for a moment that we do away with all punishment. It seems to me that this would have profound consequences for both the victim and the perpetrator of the crime. It would do away not only with retribution (which aims at satisfying a perceived need for revenge, apart from considerations about the future well-being of the community), but also with the other three goals of punishment, each of which aims at the shalom of the community. In other words, in our world punishment is necessary for the sake of restorative justice—justice that reconciles the victim, the perpetrator, and the community.

In terms of prevention and deterrence, an unequivocal rejection of punishment means at the very least that the external incentives to stop criminal behavior are being reduced. Why would people stop their criminal behavior unless they expect a legal penalty for engaging in that behavior? "Cheap grace," argues L. Gregory Jones, "denies any real need for deliverance from sin since it justifies the sin instead of the sinner. As such, cheap grace offers consolation without any change of life, without any sense of either dying or rising in Christ. Indeed, cheap grace does not require any embodiment."[40] Abolishing all external punishment eliminates a much-needed incentive for the perpetrator to stop the cycle of victimization and so removes the perpetrator's as well as the victim's hope for peace and justice.

For the victim, a nonpenal understanding of justice carries a further consequence: There is no recourse for the offense. Regardless of how little remorse the offender may show, the victim is forced to accept that society refuses to deal with the crime. The result may well be that "the world will remain forever awry, the blood of the innocent will eternally cry out to heaven."[41] Even if and when it is true that the victim of violence is obligated to extend forgiveness, experience dictates that such forgiveness is long and arduous, oftentimes not forthcoming at all. If it is to be adapted to real life, the judicial system needs to take into account the victim's difficulty in extending forgiveness to the perpetrator. The strong human propensity to harbor feelings of revenge is a reality in a sinful world: where victimizing others is not punished, this omission may aggravate the damage done by the criminal, further diminishing prospects for reconciliation. Without punishment, it becomes more difficult to mend the tears in the social fabric and to achieve justice.[42] An entirely nonpenal understanding of justice is not just, simply because it undermines the possibility of communion and so impedes eschatological justice.

It seems clear, therefore, that under certain conditions punishment can play a positive role. Rehabilitation, deterrence, and prevention may make punishment a good and necessary thing. Ultimately, the purpose of punishment is the community's well-being: the crime has affected the community's relationships, which need healing. Punishment can restore hope. To be sure, this *apologia* for punishment does not settle the question of when to punish. It does not settle the question of the appropriate degree of punishment in particular situations. The answers to these questions will always depend on *ad hoc* decisions regarding particular laws and particular people in particular circumstances.

The hypothetical justifiability of *some* form of divine punishment does not mean, therefore, that the specific punishment of Christ on the cross was appropriate. This leads us to inquire about the particularities of the Law that led to Christ's death. Interestingly, not every transgression of the Old Testament Law led to punishment. According to the Law, Israelites could atone for their sins by means of repentance and sacrifice, thereby restoring fellowship.[43] The Deuteronomic Law suggests, however, that Israel consistently rejected the very aim of repentance and sacrifice: restoration of, and growth in, her relationship with God. The book of Deuteronomy leads up to God's prediction of the rebellion of Israel, her rejection of the Shema, and thus to exile as the curse of the Law.[44] The books of Joshua through 2 Kings trace Israel's apostasy leading up to the exilic curse.[45] Significantly, exile is God's last option. He resorts to this climactic punishment only once it becomes clear that Israel as a nation has consistently refused to repent and so to obtain forgiveness from God. Exilic punishment (and Christ's suffering on the cross), we could say, is a form of restorative justice that is meant for the restoration of the people of God. The cross only makes sense in the light of the resurrection that follows it.

Atonement and the Possibility of Community

Some readers may feel that even if I have made a valiant case for a modified Reformed position, we might find it easier to live together in communities if we hold to a nonviolent view of the atonement. I do acknowledge that historically, whenever Calvinism gained the upper hand, the violence of God seemed to transfer rather easily to structures of oppression. And I am not convinced that authoritarian or oppressive structures are entirely unrelated to certain types of Reformed theology.[46] But in this chapter, I need not be concerned with scholastic Calvinism. The question is whether my modified Reformed position also undermines the love of God and leaves us with divine violence at the heart of God, thereby resulting in human communal structures that are unduly violent and oppressive.

The refusal to use coercion and to inflict harm or damage is really a refusal to enforce boundaries. To be sure, it is possible to defend the wrong boundaries. It is possible to defend the right boundaries for the wrong motives. It is also possible to enforce boundaries at too high a price. Furthermore, it is possible to forget that some boundaries are porous or fluid and should be treated as such. In other words, to speak in favor of boundary maintenance is not to justify any and all boundary maintenance. In his *Reply to Faustus the Manichaean*, Saint Augustine comments:

> The real evils in war are love of violence, revengeful cruelty, fierce and implacable enmity, wild resistance, and the lust of power, and such like; and it is generally to punish these things, when force is required to inflict the punishment, that, in obedience to God or some lawful authority, good men undertake wars, when they find themselves in such a position as regards the conduct of human affairs, that right conduct requires them to act, or to make others act in this way.[47]

Augustine decries here the *love* of violence—not every act of violence as such—as something that must be opposed. The Augustinian perspective would unequivocally condemn people engaging in violence out of purely sadistic pleasure or for the satisfaction that retribution may offer. Not all violence is justified. Marjorie Suchocki makes a similar point when she argues that violence is sinful whenever it is unnecessary.[48] Violence may be unavoidable and even morally required under certain circumstances. But it needs to be avoided and countered as much as possible. Unnecessary injury is morally reprehensible.

The problem with a nonviolent atonement theory, however, is that it leads to the negation of all boundaries. The refusal to engage in any penal violence means a refusal to engage in truly restorative justice. The reason for this is not difficult to observe. Thomas Oden, in a recent discussion on the need for boundaries, comments: "A center without a circumference is just a dot, nothing more. It is the circumference that marks the boundary of the circle. To eliminate the boundary is to eliminate the circle itself. The circle of faith cannot identify its center without recognizing its perimeter."[49] Oden is concerned that we maintain a sense of boundaries, since it is boundaries that allow us to maintain our identity. Caroline Westerhoff, likewise, speaks of *Good Fences*, insisting that to maintain one's boundaries is not a negative but a positive thing.[50] Oden and Westerhoff both apply this to the church community, with Oden being concerned with the teaching of the church and Westerhoff with the practices of the members of the church. And there is no doubt that the question of boundaries is of importance to the church. Baptism and Eucharist, for example, are practices on the boundary of the church. Questions of intercommunion between various denominations often lead to emotional discussions precisely because they are boundary issues and determinative of the community's identity.[51] The way in which we resolve questions surrounding baptism and Eucharist determines at least to a degree what kind of a community we are.

It seems no coincidence that John Milbank, Radical Orthodoxy's most prominent spokesperson, combines a nonviolent view of the atonement with a strong disregard for ecclesial boundaries. As I have argued elsewhere, Milbank looks to the church's practices of forgiveness as constituting atonement.[52] Since, according to Milbank, we ought to equate the church with Christ, it is the practices of the church that constitute reconciliation.[53] We should not say, for example, that Christ's death is "something *in addition* to the human practice of forgiveness."[54] This means that for Milbank both the Calvinist espousal of substitutionary punishment and the Liberal acceptance of the moral influence theory are suspect. Both imply far too sharp a distinction between the church and the historical Jesus. For Milbank, it is the church that accomplishes atonement in its practices of forgiveness.

This rather sharp rejection of a Reformed understanding of the atonement results in part from Milbank's apprehension of violence and punishment. His ontology is an ontology of peace. Over against both modern and postmodern construals of reality, Milbank maintains that the Christian faith tells a different story, a story of peace and harmony. Through his death on the cross, Christ makes a "totally non-violent, unconstraining" appeal to us to enter into this same participatory process of forgiveness.[55] Such a nonviolent practice of forgiveness cannot possibly go hand in hand with a penal view of the cross. Indeed, despite his admiration for Augustine, Milbank sharply criticizes his "inadequate ontology of punishment."[56] I am neither convinced, however, that Augustine holds to an "ontology of punishment" nor that all punishment is to be rejected as evil and so as nothingness (*privatio boni*). I would rather say that Augustine, as well as the just war tradition following him, is built on a carefully construed balance that maintains, on the one hand, an ontology of peace, and acknowledges, on the other hand, the need for redemptive violence, precisely for the paradoxical purpose of achieving ultimate peace and justice.

But when Augustinianism is rejected as an unfortunate "ontology of punishment" and when traditional Western atonement theories are put aside because of their rejection of the truly nonviolent ecclesial / christological processes of forgiveness, it is not surprising that we end up with an ecclesiology that does not wish to reckon with any boundaries at all. Christianity, insists Milbank, is the religion of the obliteration of boundaries and limits.[57] This obliteration has immediate ecclesial implications: for Milbank, nothing is exactly "outside" the church.[58] James K. A. Smith, in his recent book on Radical Orthodoxy, rightly questions how such a universality of the *ecclesia* fits with Milbank's countercultural agenda: "But wasn't it Milbank, in *Theology and Social Theory*, who asserted the fundamental antithesis of the *ecclesia* vis-à-vis other configurations of the *polis*—and asserted that the church alone was the site for renewed communion and sociality?"[59] But if nothing is outside the church and thus all boundaries are obliterated, one wonders how baptism and Eucharist are to function on the boundaries of the church. I will readily grant Milbank that the church's boundaries ought to be permeable. The church is to be the hospitable community par excellence. But one cannot help but wonder *which* community it is that is supposed to exercise hospitality and *which* community it is that is supposed to engage in practices of forgiveness if all attempts at identification are ultimately a lapse into an ontology of violence.

Reformed theology needs to guard against juridicizing, individualizing, and dehistoricizing the atonement. These Calvinist tendencies may well imply an inclination toward an ontology of violence that obscures the love of God. But the converse is equally true: to reject all traditional atonement theories simply because they involve divine violence leads to an obliteration of all boundaries and hence of all sense of identity. I have illustrated this by means of Milbank's view of the church. But the argument has broader applicability. Let me just give a few examples. With regard to criminal justice, to insist on retributive justice for its own sake is to inscribe violence in the heart of our communities. But to plead for a restorative justice that rejects all punishment is to open our gates and to invite chaos to take over. With regard to questions of just war, to defend the liberal democratic nation state at all cost without asking how the Western world measures up to the standards of God's kingdom is to ignore the relativity of the boundaries of Western civilization. But to plead for a pacifist or nonviolent position is to reject the good boundaries of the created order and, in Jacques Derrida's terms, to invite the devil to come in.[60]

Before concluding, I should make one final caveat. My attempt at some kind of theodicy in favor of redemptive violence is not meant to provide a logically conclusive argument that proves the necessity for divine punishment on the cross. Such an attempt would fail on at least two counts: (1) it would fail to answer satisfactorily why *this* particular punishment was necessary at *this* particular time; and (2) it would be unable to explain rationally how it is possible for God's violence and wrath not to obscure his love. Instead, I have taken my starting point in the narrative of salvation. It is a narrative in which the God of Jesus Christ employs violence for the sake of the ultimate shalom of the kingdom of God. It is only with an eye to the mystery of the absolutely nonviolent eschaton that we dare say that God does have a purpose with the crucifixion of Jesus Christ.[61] The ultimate "theodicy" of divine violence, therefore, lies in the resurrection as the completion of the Paschal mystery. Without the prospect of the overcoming of violence, the cross would remain a mere human tragedy. Redemptive violence, therefore, finds its justification not in a rationally conclusive argument but in a story of salvation that is based on an ontology of love and of peace, because the story ends in the kingdom of peace. Barbara Brown Taylor, struggling with the questions raised by divine violence and by the terror that we encounter in our lives, finally concludes: "If we are tempted to draw back from it and seek an easier way, we are not alone. The world is full of former disciples. 'Do you also wish to go away?' Jesus asks the handful who are left him in the sixth chapter of John (6:67). 'Lord,' Simon Peter answers him, 'to whom can we go? You have the words of eternal life.'"[62]

Contemporary advocates of nonviolent atonement theories posit an unfortunate disjunction with the broad tradition of Christian theology. I have tried to show why such a disjunction is unnecessary and even harmful. Arguments in favor of a nonviolent atonement typically end up being arguments that reject divine intentionality of the cross. Such a rejection of divine intentionality cannot do justice to the many biblical allusions, in both the Old and the New Testaments, to divine violence. What is more, such a rejection of divine intentionality tends toward an obliteration of boundaries and identities, which will have serious societal repercussions if left unchallenged. One of more obvious and immediate repercussions of the refusal to include punishment in the administration of justice is the abandonment of the victims of violence, so that the restoration of shalom remains elusive. Restorative justice cannot function without due regard for the need for punishment. Ironically, by cutting out the wrath and violence of God in an attempt to hold up his love, we end up losing the very thing we are trying to safeguard: the restoration of shalom and, therefore, the enjoyment of the presence of God's love. It may be true that the history of Reformed theology has displayed the opposite danger: a reification of punishment as universally necessary to uphold the justice of God is unable to uphold the priority of divine love vis-à-vis divine wrath. The result is indeed the loss of an ontology of love or of peace. But a modified Reformed atonement theology as I have outlined it in this chapter enables us to maintain the priority of divine love (with exilic punishment serving as a last resort and administered with a view to the restoration of shalom). Such a modified Reformed position is willing to take up the challenge of seeking wisdom in the everyday difficult task of boundary maintenance. We do not need to abandon the broad consensus of the Christian tradition. Especially when viewed within an overall framework of recapitulation or reconstitution, each of the three main strands of the tradition offers us elements that we can only ignore at our own peril. God's involvement in the cross is a true embodiment of his love. The Christian faith sees the evidence for this in the resurrection as the completion of the Paschal mystery.

Notes

1. Rita Nakashima Brock, *Journeys by Heart: A Christology of Erotic Power* (New York: Crossroad, 1988), 56.

2. Darby Kathleen Ray, *Deceiving the Devil: Atonement, Abuse, and Ransom* (Cleveland: Pilgrim Press, 1998), 58.

3. It is my position that strict Calvinist views of predestination and limited atonement unnecessarily limit our appreciation of the love of God. See chapter 2 of my *Violence, Hospitality, and the Cross: Reappropriating the Atonement Tradition* (Grand Rapids, MI: Baker Academic, 2004).

4. J. Denny Weaver elaborates on these three objections throughout his book *The Nonviolent Atonement* (Grand Rapids, MI: Eerdmans, 2001).

5. I give a more extensive critique of high Calvinist views in *Violence, Hospitality, and the Cross*, 163-70.

6. Cyril of Jerusalem, *Catechetical Lectures*, in *Nicene and Post-Nicene Fathers*, Second Series, trans. Edward Hamilton Gifford, ed. Philip Schaff and Henry Ware (reprint, Peabody, MA: Hendrickson, 1994), 7:89 (XIII.28). There are many such patristic texts illustrating the cosmic mystery of the cross. See Joseph Ratzinger, *The Spirit of the Liturgy*, trans. John Saward (San Francisco: Ignatius, 2000), 182-83.

7. I plan to work out some of the implications of the mystery of the incarnation in a future publication.

8. Biblical quotations in this essay are taken from the *New Jerusalem Bible*.

9. Irenaeus, *Irenaeus Against Heresies*, in *The Ante-Nicene Fathers* (hereafter *AH*), ed. Alexander Roberts and James Donaldson (1885; reprint, Peabody, MA: Hendrickson, 1994), 1:421 (III.8.2); 1:447-48 (III.18.6); 1:455-56 (III.23.1). Cf. 1:457 (III.23.7).

10. Ibid., 1:550 (V.21.3).

11. Ibid., 1:423 (III.9.3); Irenaeus, *Proof of the Apostolic Preaching* (hereafter *Dem.*),

trans. Joseph P. Smith (New York: Paulist, 1952), 31, 38; Irenaeus, *Fragments from the Lost Writings of Irenæus*, in *The Ante-Nicene Fathers* (hereafter *Frag.*), 1:575 (43).

12. See Irenaeus, *AH* 1:457 (III.23.7); 1:548 (V.21.1).

13. Gregory of Nyssa, *The Great Catechism*, in *Nicene and Post-Nicene Fathers*, Second Series, trans. William Moore and Henry Austin Wilson, ed. Philip Schaff and Henry Wace (1893; reprint, Peabody, MA: Hendrickson, 1994), 5:494 (XXIV).

14. Ibid., 5:495 (XXVI).

15. Ibid., 5:496 (XXVI).

16. Indeed, both Irenaeus and Gregory of Nyssa argue against divine violence in redemption. According to Irenaeus, apostasy used deception and violence whereby "it insatiably snatched away what was not its own." By contrast, God uses "persuasion" instead of "violent means" and does not infringe upon "justice" (See *AH* 1:457 [III.23.7]; 1:527 [V.1.1]; 1:548 [V.21.1]). Nyssa, in similar fashion, develops his fishhook or deception theory in opposition to divine violence.

17. Cf. Weaver, *Nonviolent Atonement*, 73.

18. This understanding of persuasion as involving violence asks for a definition of violence, which I discuss below.

19. In the few biblical passages that I have referred to above, I have only spoken of divine intentionality in connection with the cross. I have left out of the discussion the numerous references to divine violence in both the Old and the New Testaments.

20. Rita Nakashima Brock and Rebecca Ann Parker, *Proverbs of Ashes: Violence, Redemptive Suffering, and the Search for What Saves Us* (Boston: Beacon Press, 2001), 49.

21. Weaver, *Nonviolent Atonement*, 73.

22. Ibid., 226.

23. For an argument pleading for an Irenaean reading of Ephesians 1:10, see John McHugh, "A Reconsideration of Ephesians 1.10b in the Light of Irenaeus," in *Paul and Paulinism: Essays in Honour of C. K. Barrett*, ed. M. D. Hooker and S. G. Wilson (London: SPCK, 1982), 302-9.

24. I am open to referring to this representation as vicarious or substitutionary as long as it is clear that Christ is not simply replacing human beings as a third party, but includes all others in his recapitulation, so that it really is a reconstitution of Adamic humanity itself in Jesus Christ.

25. Irenaeus, *AH* 1:448 (III.18.7); 1:454 (III.21.10); *Dem.* 32.

26. Irenaeus therefore mines the temptation narratives for analogies between Christ and Adam (*AH* 1:548-50 [V.21.1-3]). Cf. D. Jeffrey Bingham, *Irenaeus' Use of Matthew's Gospel in Adversus Haereses*; Traditio Exegetica Graeca, no. 7 (Leuven: Peeters, 1998), 274-81.

27. Irenaeus, *AH* 1:545 (V.17.2). Cf. 1:544 (V.16.3); 1:545 (V.17.3); 1:547 (V.19.1); *Dem.* 34; *Frag.* 1:28.

28. For a fuller exposition of how Irenaeus works out each of these three elements, see Hans Boersma, "Redemptive Hospitality in Irenaeus: A Model for Ecumenicity in a Violent World," *Pro Ecclesia* 11 (2002): 207-26.

29. See, for instance, N. T. Wright, *Jesus and the Victory of God*, vol. 2, *Christian Origins and the Question of God* (Minneapolis: Fortress Press, 1996), 169.

30. And since, through original sin, all humans are implicated in Adam's sin, this Calvinist theological framework regards it as by definition impossible for anyone to observe the Law.

31. Galatians 3:10: "On the other hand, all those who depend on the works of the Law are under a curse, since scripture says: *Accursed be he who does not make what is written in the book of the Law effective, by putting it into practice* [Deut. 27:26]."

32. My understanding of Galatians 3:10-14 has been deeply influenced by N. T. Wright, *The Climax of the Covenant: Christ and the Law in Pauline Theology* (Minneapolis: Fortress Press, 1992), 137-56. I have given a detailed exposition in *Violence, Hospitality, and the Cross*, 171-77.

33. Donald X. Burt gives this example in *Friendship and Society: An Introduction to Augustine's Practical Philosophy* (Grand Rapids, MI: Eerdmans, 1999), 164.

34. Weaver, *Nonviolent Atonement*, 8-9.

35. Walter Wink, *Engaging the Powers: Discernment and Resistance in a World of Domination* (Minneapolis: Fortress Press, 1984), 216. Italics in original.

36. Ibid., 192. Italics in original.

37. Ibid., 227.

38. Wink's suggestion that the victory of counterviolence might "usher in a better society" (Ibid., 224) directly clashes with his notion that all violence is mimetic in character and as such always self-defeating.

39. Burt, *Friendship and Society*, 185-86.

40. L. Gregory Jones, *Embodying Forgiveness: A Theological Analysis* (Grand Rapids, MI: Eerdmans, 1995), 13.

41. Miroslav Volf, *Exclusion and Embrace: A Theological Exploration of Identity, Otherness, and Reconciliation* (Nashville: Abingdon Press, 1996), 294.

42. Of course, one might argue that if the perpetrator repents, forgiveness rather than punishment should be forthcoming. The question is, however: Whose forgiveness? A third party extending forgiveness on behalf of the victim is usually problematic, and it is hardly the judge's right to forgive a crime.

43. Compare John H. Hayes, "Atonement in the Book of Leviticus," *Interpretation* 52 (1998): 10-12; E. P. Sanders, *Paul and Palestinian Judaism: A Comparison of Patterns of Religion* (Philadelphia: Fortress Press, 1977), 157-82. It will be clear that also in this respect my Reformed position is a modified one. For high Calvinism, every sin committed against God necessitates eternal divine punishment and therefore Christ's death on the cross.

44. Deuteronomy 28:32, 36-37, 49-52, 63-68; 29:28; 31:16-22, 29. The Song of Moses that the Israelites are to sing (Deut. 32) is to function as a self-indictment.

45. Gordon McConville, *Grace in the End: A Study in Deuteronomic Theology* (Grand Rapids, MI: Zondervan, 1993), 65-122.

46. Although the following two books are rather one-sided, they do illustrate the danger of a strong emphasis on retributive justice: Timothy Gorringe, *God's Just Vengeance: Crime, Violence and the Rhetoric of Salvation* (Cambridge: Cambridge University Press, 1996); Richard T. Snyder, *The Protestant Ethic and the Spirit of Punishment* (Grand Rapids, MI: Eerdmans, 2001).

47. Saint Augustine, *Reply to Faustus the Manichæan*, trans. Richard Stothert, vol. 4 of *Nicene and Post-Nicene Fathers*, First Series, ed. Philip Schaff (1887; Peabody, MA: Hendrickson, 1994), 301 (XXII.74).

48. Marjorie Hewitt Suchocki, *The Fall to Violence: Original Sin in Relational Theology* (New York: Continuum, 1994), 95.

49. Thomas C. Oden, *The Rebirth of Orthodoxy: Signs of New Life in Christianity* (SanFrancisco: HarperSanFrancisco, 2002), 131.

50. Caroline Westerhoff, *Good Fences: The Boundaries of Hospitality* (Cambridge, MA: Cowley, 1999).

51. See my essay, "Liturgical Hospitality: Theological Reflections on Sharing in Grace," *Journal for Christian Theological Research* 8 (2003): 67-77. Cf. also James Farwell, "Baptism, Eucharist, and the Hospitality of Jesus: On the Practice of 'Open Communion,'" *Anglican Theological Review* 86 (2004): 215-38.

52. Hans Boersma, "Being Reconciled: Cultural-Ecclesial Practice as Atonement in Radical Orthodoxy," in *Radical Orthodoxy and the Reformed Tradition: Creation, Covenant, and Participation*, ed. James K. A. Smith and James H. Olthuis (Grand Rapids, MI: Baker Academic, 2005).

53. John Milbank speaks, for instance, of an "ecclesiological construal of Christ's divine personhood, which regards Christ as having arrived only in terms of his final, eschatological arrival which is yet to come" (*The Word Made Strange: Theology, Language, Culture* [Malden, U.K.: Blackwell, 1997], 159).

54. Ibid. (emphasis added)

55. Ibid., 141.

56. John Milbank, *Theology and Social Theory: Beyond Secular Reason* (Oxford: Blackwell, 1990), 421.

57. John Milbank, *Being Reconciled: Ontology and Pardon* (London: Routledge, 2003), 196.

58. Ibid., 121.

59. James K. A. Smith, *Introducing Radical Orthodoxy: Toward a Post-Secular Worldview* (Grand Rapids, MI: Baker Academic, 2004), 258.

60. Unfortunately, Derrida explicitly advocates a rejection of boundaries and insists we must accept that the devil may come in. Cf. Jacques Derrida, "Hospitality, Justice and Responsibility: A Dialogue with Jacques Derrida," in *Questioning Ethics: Contemporary Debates in Philosophy*, ed. Richard Kearney and Mark Dooley (London: Routledge, 1999), 70.

61. The notion of an absolutely nonviolent eschaton raises difficult questions, at least if we want to affirm the continuation of God's good creation in the hereafter. If the created order, as we know it, necessarily involves boundaries and *hence* violence, wouldn't this imply the presence of violence also in the eschaton? Perhaps the best way to deal with this thorny question is to say that we need both the kataphatic affirmation of the presence of boundaries in the eschaton, and also an apophaticism that says that this eschatological boundary involves an epistemic limitation for us, so that we cannot explain *how* boundaries can have a place in an absolutely nonviolent eschaton. We have to paradoxically affirm both eschatological realities: continuation of time and matter *and* the existence of matter in such a way that all violence will have disappeared. I have worked out this proposal in more detail in "Irenaeus, Derrida and Hospitality: On the Eschatological Overcoming of Violence," *Modern Theology* 19 (2003): 163-80.

62. Barbara Brown Taylor, "Preaching the Terrors," in *Exilic Preaching: Testimony for Christian Exiles in an Increasingly Hostile Culture*, ed. Erskine Clarke (Harrisburg, PA: Trinity Press International, 1998), 90.

RESPONSES TO
HANS BOERSMA

Response to Hans Boersma
J. Denny Weaver

General Observations

Hans Boersma and I agree on at least one central issue, namely that standard or traditional atonement theories enshrine or depend on violence, and have been used in ways that further violence. Boersma validates much of the analysis of theologians such as Rita Nakashima Brock and myself that has exposed the embedded violence within standard atonement theories. However, our responses to that intrinsic violence in standard atonement theology differ greatly. Boersma provides a "modified reformed view" of atonement that retains but limits and somewhat camouflages the violence of atonement under the image of recapitulation and reconstitution, while also affirming the general utility of violence in the practical realm. In contrast, my proposal develops an image of atonement, namely narrative *Christus Victor*, which does not depend on violence, which reflects the rejection of violence in the narrative of Jesus, and which serves as the theological foundation for nonviolent ethics modeled on the life of Jesus. This debate concerns not only atonement theology. It goes to the heart of the discussion about the nature of Christian faith and practice.

Several interrelated observations highlight additional dimensions of this discussion.

1. Boersma and I agree that the atonement of Christ involves violence. We disagree on whose violence it is. Boersma attributes it ultimately to God, whereas I lay it fully at the feet of humankind.

2. Stated differently, Boersma is trying to hold together the conundrum of satisfaction atonement in which God somehow needs the death of Jesus while the people who kill Jesus are resisting the reign of God in Jesus who is obedient to God; but the people who kill Jesus also are fulfilling God's intent that Jesus die to accomplish salvation. This conundrum is

the result of Anselm's removal of the devil from the atonement discussion. Boersma's solution is to call violence good; my solution is to restore the "devil" to the equation.

3. Beyond discussions about the death of Jesus, the larger issue of atonement concerns the image of the God who works in Jesus. The God Boersma imagines uses violence; my image of God does not depend on or sanction violence.

4. One can pose these questions in terms of divine intentionality. Boersma believes that it was God's intention that Jesus die, which means that God uses violence. I dispute that view of God's intentionality. My view of divine intention is that God intended for Jesus to give a life-affirming and life-giving witness to the reign of God. Rather than understanding Jesus' death as a divine necessity, I see it as the world's response to the reign of God made present in the life of Jesus. Jesus' death is that which distinguishes the modus operandi of the reign of God from that of the rule of evil.

5. Boersma's view ensconces violence at every turn. My atonement image rejects divinely sanctioned violence. Ultimately the basis of this rejection of divine violence is christological and trinitarian—if God is fully revealed in Jesus, as Christian theology represented by Nicene and trinitarian doctrine professes, then the God who is revealed in and fully present in the life of Jesus cannot be a God who espouses violence.

Some Particular Rejoinders

Since the basis of my analysis of atonement violence is already contained in my essay in this volume, the response in this section is limited to calling attention to particular points for emphasis and to correcting what I perceive to be errors and misperceptions in Boersma's essay.

Narrative *Christus Victor*, the atonement model I propose, depends on or is a theological derivative of the narrative of the life of Jesus culminating with the resurrection, and it is a carrying forward of the imagery of Revelation in portraying the meaning of the life, death, and resurrection of Jesus. This image has clear ethical connotations. Its understanding of the saved life of the Christian assumes that the believer is a disciple of

Jesus, and that the Christian life is then lived in ways shaped by the non-violent life of Jesus.

Typical of the standard theories of atonement, Boersma's modified Reformed view says little if anything about the life of Jesus and focuses primarily on the death of Jesus. It is this death that is involved when Boersma defends divine intentionality in the death of Jesus. His mention of resurrection comes when including a *Christus Victor* motif under the guise that recapitulation can encompass all atonement views. The ethical connotation of this violence-assuming atonement image is that Christians continue to use violence, whether judicially or militarily. His view portrays the continuing attraction and fascination with violence that characterizes so much of the Western world.

Boersma's intention to combine aspects of the three standard atonement images ignores my argument that distinguishes these theories in terms of the object or "target" of the death of Jesus. Tracking the object of the death shows that the death is aimed in quite different directions—toward Satan, toward God or God's law, and toward sinful humankind—which makes them conceptually incompatible with one another. Further, the historical relationship of the theories renders them incompatible, with Anselm rejecting *Christus Victor* and removing the devil from the equation, and Abelard then redirecting the death of Jesus from God to aim it at humankind. To keep all three theories requires either doing violence to the inner logic of Anselm and Abelard under the guise of keeping these theories or in effect rendering systematic inquiry meaningless in the development of atonement theology.

Boersma makes a strong appeal to the broad Christian tradition. Appeal to tradition is fraught with problems, however. Why are we obligated to follow the particular Reformed tradition that Boersma chooses? If the ancestors of that Reformed tradition had heeded the call to follow tradition in the sixteenth century, Boersma would still be Catholic. In any case, if the Bible is truly the beginning point for theology, then we should be in a perpetual reforming mode, always returning again to the Bible's story. This return to the Bible is not a call or a claim to be able to ignore tradition or the long series of answers throughout Christian history, but it does mean that if the Bible is truly authoritative then a particular historical tradition should not be granted the authority to define a particular reading of the Bible as the necessary or the only acceptable reading.

Boersma quoted several biblical texts to prove divine intentionality in the death of Jesus. In my view, he brings a presumption of violence and divine violence to such texts. If one does not read the New Testament through an Anselmian-focused lens, and reads without a presumption in favor of divine violence, it is possible to read all of these texts in ways that do not teach and advocate a view of divine violence.

Boersma's discussion of definitions of violence and coercion raises a very important issue. However, I dispute his conclusion. I agree with Boersma in observing differing levels or degrees of violence and of coercion. My disagreement concerns how we classify these levels of coercion and violence. The presumed logical approach, so transparent that it is never justified and barely recognized, is to arrange the options in order along a continuum, from the least to the most—such as least to most violence used. At one end of the spectrum would be passive nonresistance with the most forceful, lethal violence at the other end. As Boersma apparently understands the options along the continuum, except for passive nonresistance at the one end, every position on this continuum is some level of violence. He locates what I would call nonviolent coercion or nonviolent resistance on this continuum and labels it "violence." Various actions of Jesus, from transgressing Sabbath laws by healing to the temple cleansing are on this continuum—and identified as violence. However, I reject Boersma's claim that all such acts are violence. Indeed, I dispute the common assumption that all acts involving coercion of any kind belong on the same continuum.

If we have eyes focused by the rejection of violence in the narrative of Jesus, a second continuum comes into view. A primary characteristic of this continuum is that it rejects the use of harmful coercion or lethal violence. Like the first continuum, this second continuum has passive nonresistance at one end. But in its seeking for justice and security, it refuses to participate in violence. This continuum can visualize varying levels of acceptable coercion both mental and physical, with increasing levels of intensity, but in every case it rejects the idea of inflicting lethal harm, and is willing to suffer harm rather than to inflict harm. One can arrange Jesus' actions on this continuum: using provocative and sarcastic language (Luke 11:40, 44, 52, and so forth); breaking public order by healing the withered hand on the Sabbath when he could have waited until the next day (Luke 6:6-11); traveling through Samaria and accepting a drink from a Samaritan woman, both acts that were proscribed by the purity code of his day; and a vigorous protest of corruption in the temple (Luke 19:45-46). Contemporary examples of increasing tension might go from writing the United States president a letter against the war in Iraq to sending relief supplies to Iraq in defiance of a U.S. embargo. Actions between the ends of the continuum might be: holding a demonstration if the police issue a parade permit; holding a demonstration without a permit; and breaking laws in civil disobedience, as when the Berrigans entered an air base illegally and pounded on bombers to act out turning swords into plowshares. The important thing to see is that on this second continuum, nonviolent coercion is not a compromise with violent coercion; it is not a way station along the path to lethal force. Boersma "teased" me with the idea of a nonviolent war. It is actually a nonviolent struggle. But I tease in return by asking why he is so intent on defending violence when there is a conceptual option much more in tune with the narrative of Jesus. Even though it is entirely unnecessary, Boersma chooses to define a host of actions as violent, including actions from the narrative of Jesus.

Boersma preserves the idea of divine violence because he believes it necessary in order to have a concept of divine judgment. I dispute that assumption. Judgment, a violent judgment, need not be understood as the point in divine time when God stops being patient and moves to punish. Rather judgment, violent judgment, is what evil does to itself. Biblical proclamations of divine judgment are really declarations of what evildoers will bring or have brought on themselves if they continue in their evil ways. A human analogy is the professor who warns a student that he will fail the course if he refuses to do the required assignments. The student who does not do the work may complain that a hostile and judgmental professor failed him, but in truth the student failed himself. Or think of the parable of the prodigal son. The father does not appear as a stern judge who out of righteous indignation demanded reparations or punishment before the prodigal could be returned to the bosom of the family. But from the response of the older brother, it would appear that these are precisely the kind of things that he thinks should happen. Thus in the responses of the father and the older brother, we see two very different attitudes toward forgiveness, with the father of the story imaging divine forgiveness that acknowledges repentance but does not depend on punishment.

This parable leads to a comment on Boersma's problematic understanding of restorative justice. Boersma wrote that in a "nonpenal understanding of justice...there is no recourse for the offense." A bit later, he wrote that nonviolent atonement theory "leads to negation of all boundaries." I dispute both these assertions. The goal of restorative justice is to restore the relationship between offended and offender, which includes to the extent possible restoring that which was lost. Offenders do not immediately, if ever, recognize the implications of their offense. In such cases, sanctions are important and appropriate. Boersma would call these sanctions "violence" and put them in the category of "penalty." I am here calling them "sanctions" to emphasize that one can discuss limits and "punishment" that functions for the purpose of producing change without necessarily conceptualizing these sanctions in terms of punishment that satisfies the demand for violence in retributive justice. Nonviolent resistance, as located on the second continuum described above, is quite capable of defining limits and imposing sanctions whose goal is to bring an offender to recognize the injustice of his behavior.

Boersma pictures a problem of continuity between an "absolutely nonviolent eschaton" and "a narrative in which the God of Jesus Christ employs violence for the sake of the ultimate shalom of the kingdom of God." His note 61 seems to add to this problem even further by implying that God's good creation includes the violence necessary to maintain boundaries. Alongside the discussion in the previous paragraph about whether violence is conceptually necessary in order to maintain boundaries, I suggest that there is a different reading of creation and the narrative of God's saving work in Christ that is nonviolent from creation to eschaton. When the two creation narratives of Genesis 1 and 2 are compared with the Babylonian epic the *Enuma Elish*, it becomes apparent that the two biblical stories present nonviolent creation. In *Enuma Elish*, the creation of earth and human beings is the aftermath of violent rebellion and blood vengeance among the gods, which contrasts markedly to the nonviolent images of the biblical God who creates through speaking and making sculptures. When it appears in the story, violence is the product of human disobedience and not an intrinsic part of creation.

Throughout the following story of God working with God's people in the narrative of the Old Testament, violence abounds, as is well known. Less recognized, however, is another trajectory, one of minimal violence, and involving what today would be called nonviolent resistance. Just a few examples are: Isaac's response to theft of his wells; Gideon's rout of the Midianites with three hundred unarmed men; Samuel's opposition to the idea of kingship; the cultural resistance of the Hebrew exiles in the book of Daniel; and more. The obvious question then arises whether it is the violent or the nonviolent trajectory of stories that most reflects the will of God. The answer, I believe, resides in the narrative of Jesus. If God is fully revealed in Jesus, as Christian faith proclaims, then the God of Jesus cannot be a God who uses or sanctions violence. There is indeed a nonviolent trajectory throughout the entire Bible that begins in creation, passes through Jesus, and ends in the nonviolent eschaton.

As I wrote in my essay in this volume, understanding God in terms of the narrative of Jesus is an application of traditional trinitarian thought. According to the classic understanding, there is nothing in any person of the Trinity that is not in the Godhead, nor is there anything in the Godhead that is not present in each of the three persons. If that traditional profession is accepted, then a God who uses violence is incompatible with Jesus' rejection of violence. If God is fully revealed in Jesus, then God must be nonviolent.

There is a fundamental disagreement between Hans Boersma and myself on the understanding of atonement and on the work and image of God. This disagreement centers on attitudes toward violence and its compatibility with Christian faith and practice. Boersma is determined to defend violence and to demonstrate the compatibility of violence with Christian theology and ethics. My intent is to show the incompatibility of violence with the life and teaching of Jesus and with subsequent understandings of God revealed in Jesus. As a conclusion, I simply ask, which of these views does most closely follow the narrative of Jesus that one reads in the Gospels?

Response to Hans Boersma
Thomas Finger

Among the authors in this volume, Boersma alone insists that atonement involves a direct exercise of divine violence.[1] He is also the only author to champion the substitutionary model, rejected unequivocally by Weaver and, at least rhetorically, by Daniels. However, Boersma graciously acknowledges that his Reformed tradition has sometimes expressed this view poorly, and seeks to remedy this.

Boersma, like me, finds some value in all three traditional models. Unlike me, he seeks to show that moral influence and *Christus Victor* also involve divine violence. He considers the deception and persuasion often associated with the latter to be violent, though I cannot see why. For Boersma, the Father's sending of the Son and the Son's willingness to suffer, found in both these models, also entail divine violence. But as I have tried to show, the violence to which these decisions led was not *directly* exercised by the Father.

Boersma then appropriates a major *Christus Victor* theme, drawing on Irenaeus as I do: Jesus as the human who recapitulates the journey intended for Adam and Eve. Jesus accomplishes this by obedience to God, and when he "fights the powers of evil, expels demons, withstands satanic temptation to the point of death, and rises victorious from the grave (*Christus Victor*)."[2]

With this turn to Jesus' history, Boersma reaches what he calls the starting point of his theological construction, "the narrative of salvation,"[3] which the other essays also stress. He connects Jesus with Israel's prior history, and calls him "the representative," not of some abstract humanity, but "of Israel and Adam."[4] Boersma claims that Jesus' historical representation was, in part, "penal," but shows convincingly that his approach avoids the "juridicizing, individualizing, and dehistoricizing" of some Reformed accounts of substitution.[5]

To accomplish this, Boersma enlists N. T. Wright, and considers a favorite Reformed text, about Jesus bearing "the curse of the Law" (Gal. 3:10). According to Wright, Jesus recapitulated Israel's exile and return. The penal curse that he bore, therefore, was Israel's punishment of exile, not eternal punishment for breaking some general law. However, exile, in my view, provides a prime instance of God's *indirect* punishment—by abandoning, or handing over, Israel to its enemies—not of *direct* divine violence.

Even if Boersma spots divine violence in the Jesus narrative (which I question), he misses those key episodes, central to the other three essays, where nonviolence appears at atonement's heart—where Jesus overcame Satan and his allies precisely through his nonviolent response to their violence. Had Boersma followed Wright further, he would have to deal with the way Wright places Jesus' struggle between being a warrior Messiah or a peaceful Messiah at the heart of his work, as I do. Boersma also does not consider the claim that the powers were finally judged by Jesus' nonviolent response to their crucifying cruelty, illumined by his resurrection.

Having pursued biblical narrative to a point where Jesus allegedly bore divine violence, Boersma shifts his focus to a very general, more abstract plane. He asks why many theologians reject nonviolence. He attributes it to their assumption that "violence is universally reprehensible." Boersma also asks why they find Jesus the "ultimate embodiment of nonviolence." He answers, similarly: because they call any coercive act that people consider reprehensible "violent."[6] However, Daniels and I have answered quite differently: because biblical narrative itself shows us these things.

I find it unclear whether Weaver begins, systematically, from biblical narrative or from assumptions like those that Boersma identifies. Such assumptions appear to operate as axiomatic presuppositions quite often, from Weaver's first paragraph on. Weaver adds that his "narrative *Christus Victor* is *grounded in* assumptions of nonviolence."[7] To the extent that he simply adopts such assumptions, and defines violence merely as "harm or damage,"[8] Weaver opens himself to Boersma's general criticisms, since we all consider some acts that harm some creatures beneficial.

In the second half of his essay, Boersma's arguments are more often sociopolitical than biblical. To counter his opponents' alleged premise, "violence is universally reprehensible," Boersma posits that violence either is sometimes necessary for social well-being, or that it never is. He then reduces the latter to absurdity.

Such a jump from Jesus' history to general sociopolitical considerations is a fairly common Reformed move. Even if some nonviolent features of that history have been noticed, this leap obscures their social implications. It does not follow biblical narrative from Jesus' nonviolent

81

behavior to the community he founded. Pacifists usually take this route, and nearly always acknowledge that violence is sometimes necessary for social well-being. But this leads to a conclusion that many Reformed find disconcerting: Christians should never exercise this violence.

To be sure, if nonviolent churches are to pursue their mission in society, and not simply withdraw, they must consider many issues that Boersma raises (and many do consider them). They must ask: How can God, in some sense, endorse rulers who employ violence (e.g., Rom. 13:1-8, 1 Pet. 2:13-17)? *Christus Victor* provides an answer. God endorses them *indirectly*, much as God permits Jesus' sufferings: by allowing rulers in their drive for power, which must aim at some measure of social stability, to further God's overall purposes. But this conclusion can also be disconcerting: it means that direct participation in government's violent functions is collusion with powers like those that crucified Jesus.

This kind of nonviolent atonement theory, at least, hardly "leads to the negation of all boundaries."[9] On the contrary, it establishes many boundaries between the church and the rest of society, and is often critiqued for this. It calls all Christians to refrain from not only violence, but also things like adversarial courts and government oaths, and to participate in mutual discipline and to share their wealth sacrificially.

In sum, I appreciate Boersma's candid critique of his own tradition, his creative reformulation of a basically substitutionary model, and his stated intent to prioritize biblical narrative. Nevertheless, his essay considers few themes in the narratives of Jesus and the early church that are central to most nonviolent theologies, and seldom, in my view, approaches the heart of their argument.

Notes

1. Boersma, 47.
2. Ibid., 55.
3. Ibid., 64-65.
4. Ibid., 55.
5. Ibid., 56.
6. Ibid., 57.
7. Weaver, 25 (italics mine).
8. Ibid., 2.
9. Boersma, 62.

Response to Hans Boersma
T. Scott Daniels

Several years ago I was participating in a big Easter musical that was being performed over several nights at a large church. Typical of most Easter pageants, at one point in the musical the choir reenacted the dramatic scene when Pilate—Jesus at his side—confronts the angry mob. On opening night when Pilate asked the poorly robed mob what we wanted him to do with this man, in our nervousness we sort of halfheartedly mumbled, "Crucify him."

The bald, heavyset church treasurer playing Pilate was visibly unimpressed by the mob, but he proceeded to wash his hands of the situation on cue. Afterward the choir director was very upset with the "wimpiness" of the mob and encouraged us to become much more aggressive the following evening.

When our cue came the next evening, we were ready. In response to Pilate's question, we screamed, contorted our faces, jumped up and down, waved our arms, and shouted at the top of our lungs, "Crucify him! Crucify him!" In that graphic—if admittedly over-the-top—moment I realized that I was acting out my deepest understandings of the atonement. When I attempt to narrate myself into the accounts of the crucifixion, I inevitably find myself among the mob shouting curses of rejection against the incarnate one.

It may sound simplistic, but the question I wrestle with regarding any form—modified or not—of substitutionary atonement is this: Is God the Father also among the mob demanding, even requiring, the crucifixion of the Son? Is he too condemning the innocent one and letting the guilty go free?

In his articulate essay, Boersma repeatedly speaks of and tries to defend "divine intentionality" with regards to a Reformed or substitutionary view of the atonement. Although I have great appreciation for what Boersma is attempting to do, I do not find the term *intentionality* to be overly helpful for getting at the heart of the real critique by (so-called) nonviolent advocates of substitution or penal satisfaction theories. I do not believe that most advocates of nonviolent atonement theories question whether or not there is any divine intention to the cross (the alternative apparently being that the divine presence uniquely found in the person of Christ *unintentionally* participates in the crucifixion). It seems to me that the primary question raised regarding substitutionary atonement is not divine *intention*—Does the divine presence participate?—but divine *participation*—How does the divine participate in the cross?

Boersma is correct in stating, "Each of the three traditional atonement models—*Christus Victor,* moral influence, and penal substitution—interpret the cross as the result also of divine intentionality."[1] However, the first two theories have an entirely different location, and thus a very different intentionality than the latter. Though I would certainly like to do some modifying to both the *Christus Victor* and the moral influence theories, they both clearly place the location of the divine presence with the victims of violence. The strength of the moral influence theory is that by locating the presence of the kingdom in the weakness and vulnerability of the suffering Christ, it makes intelligible the call to the disciple's cross.[2] We are influenced to identify with those who suffer because it is among the oppressed that we find the unique divine presence. Likewise, the strength of the *Christus Victor* model—modified to see the "powers" in terms closer to Wink than Irenaeus—is that the suffering divine presence unmasks and thus exposes the violent forces of power responsible for the crucifixion.

Although the substitutionary model locates the divine presence with the one punished, it also continues to locate the divine presence with the punisher. Thus the issue I continue to stumble over—even in the modified version by Boersma—is that I believe it was the divine intention to die, but was it the divine intention to kill?

The following questions and comments also linger for me:

1. Any version of the substitutionary atonement theory depends at least in part on the sacrificial system for a framework of interpretation. Boersma makes reference to several texts that he believes are ignored by proponents of nonviolence. But any scriptural argument for substitution also has to contend with the multiple passages in the prophets and elsewhere (for example, Isa. 1) that seem to call into question the very necessity for sacrificial death as a requirement of divine justice.

2. Boersma accuses the advocates of nonviolent atonement of being "out of step with the broad Christian tradition." It is my experience that most nonviolent atonement theorists hold to some modified versions of moral influence and *Christus Victor*—which are certainly a major part of the broader tradition. I would also argue that substitution is in many ways the exclusive product of a very narrow Western and juridical worldview. It would seem that nonviolent understandings of atonement have much in common with the more relational or "therapeutic" views of the gospel found in the Eastern tradition. Perhaps maintaining an exclusive Western dogma-

tism (even if you have to modify it and throw out important doctrines of Reformed theology to do it) is a little out of step with the broader tradition.

3. I am not sure that I concur with Boersma's interpretation of the "curse of the Law" from Galatians. If I understand Pauline theology correctly, I do not believe Paul is arguing that Christ's punishment on the cross freed us from the curse of the Law (which in a substitutionary understanding would be God's wrath), but that it is the injustice of Christ's death that destroyed the Law. In other words, Paul seems to argue that the Law is dead not because Christ somehow fulfilled its requirements, but because the Law proved itself as ultimately incapable of bringing salvation because it convicted even Christ—the innocent and divine one—to death as a lawbreaker.

4. I am not sure that I would share Boersma's interpretation of exile as a form of restorative justice for the people of God. I think I would rather understand exile as the natural consequence of Israel's decision to be just like all the other nations. Once Israel chose to line up in the valley with all the other powers (Joel 3) they were not only required to compete with those powers, but they also became subject to them when they were overthrown.

I have several other questions, but I will stop there because this last question summarizes my continual struggle with any substitutionary view. Boersma admits that he is not trying to prove the *necessity* for divine punishment, but it seems to me that once the divine presence is no longer exclusively located on the cross—suffering at the hands of violent humanity, identifying with the forsaken exiles of history, and exposing the true nature of the powers—but also finds itself looking on with the condemning crowd, the questions of particularity have to be answered satisfactorily for a theory of substitution to be maintained. And I have not yet seen a persuasive rationality for the necessity of divine punishment. I admit that as a non-Reformed Christian I don't have the stake in maintaining the particular tradition that Boersma is working to uphold, and so my view is skewed a bit. I can agree with him that we see in the cross the divine intention to die, but I still struggle to glimpse in the "crucified God" the intention to kill.

Notes

1   Boersma, 51.

2. As I point out in my chapter "Passing the Peace," one of the great weaknesses of the substitutionary tradition is that the call for the disciple to take up the cross makes little sense if the cross is simply the location of divine justice.

CHRISTUS VICTOR AS NONVIOLENT ATONEMENT

Thomas Finger

I f the issue of atonement and nonviolence is ever relevant, no time would seem more likely than the present. Violence in our cities and in conflicts around the globe spills across our television screens. Weaponry sufficient to annihilate humankind several times over has formed an ominous, silent backdrop of our existence for decades. Increasingly today, explosive, violent terror strikes without warning or regard for most of its victims to further political aims. Powerful nations, when attacked in this way, often respond with technologically sophisticated violence. Debates rage over whether this reduces or increases the likelihood of terrorist attacks.

Throughout their histories, churches and their members have often had to wrestle with violence, not only in its criminal forms, but also with its governmental and military uses, and with questions about their participation in the last two. Responses have ranged all the way from overt promotion to tacit compliance to principled opposition to one or both of these uses of force. But despite the impact of violence on Christian life, theologians have seldom connected it with central doctrines, such as atonement. Comments on governmental and military violence usually appeared, if at all, under headings like church and state, considered somewhat distant from theology's core.

Nonviolence, if it was mentioned, was usually critiqued or else defined too narrowly to touch on "realistic" civic and military issues. This narrowing often began by assuming that nonviolence was based almost entirely on several teachings of Jesus.[1] The significance of these teachings was then restricted to either (1) personal, as opposed to sociopolitical, conduct; (2) wholly to a future age; or (3) the status of ideals that stimulate ethical behavior, but cannot be fully practiced.

The disjunction of violence from core doctrines seems surprising when we consider "atonement's" meaning. It literally means at-one-ment. Atonement can refer to all ways in which creatures and God become united. Its range is usually restricted, however: on the creaturely side, to human beings; and on the divine side, to the work of God's Son. Many acts could be included in his work (for example, incarnation, life, teachings, exorcisms, death, resurrection, ascension, present reign, intercession, return, and future reign). Atonement, however, is often further narrowed to his death. "Atonement," that is, often means theories about Jesus' cross. And then, again surprisingly, the violence involved in this seldom receives much attention.

But what if nonviolence were linked to so central a theme as atonement? What if it were integral to the way that Jesus brought, brings, and will bring at-one-ment, and to what it means for humans, even the whole creation, to be at-oned? In that case, nonviolence could not be easily dismissed as Christians seek for guidance in our increasingly violent world.

Models of Atonement

In Western Christianity, atonement theology has been much affected by two main models, often called the substitutionary and moral influence theories. My main aim is to show that a third model, the *Christus Victor*, more prominent in Eastern Christianity, can better articulate the relevant biblical materials, and can place nonviolence at atonement's center.[2] In closing I will indicate more concretely how this model can help us deal with escalating violence today.

To explain *Christus Victor*, I will often compare it with the substitutionary and moral influence models. It will be helpful, then, to briefly describe these two Western approaches and the place of all three models in theology today. To help readers grasp their broad significance, my outlines must be very general and may not strictly apply to some nuances in some versions.

The substitutionary model was classically formulated by Anselm of Canterbury (1033–1109).[3] Humans, in this model, were created to honor God, or to obey God's law. If they perfectly obeyed, they would merit a reward: eternal life. However, every person broke this law and forfeited eternal life. We deserve, instead, the penalty of eternal death. Jesus' work substituted for our failures. His obedient life merited the reward of eternal life. His cross paid the penalty of eternal death. If we accept his work for us, his payment and his merits are transferred, or imputed, to us, or to our account. We are exempted from eternal death and receive the reward of eternal life. This model conceptualizes atonement's main features in legal terms.

The moral influence theory was formulated by Peter Abelard (1079–1142), but exerted its greatest impact in nineteenth-century Protestant liberal theology.[4] Liberalism tended to explain things in terms of historical forces—conceived as moral, social, and physical processes—which is often called *historicism*. Humans, in liberal versions of this model, were created to join in moral endeavor leading to the kingdom of God, conceived largely in social and earthly terms. This is best guided by inspiration and teaching, and motivated by awareness of God's love. Through his life, Jesus provided a superb moral example and teaching and manifested divine love. His death was a supreme expression of this love, which motivates people to live for God's kingdom.

In nineteenth-century North America, evangelical Protestants, somewhat like liberal Protestants, sought to advance God's kingdom and undertook social ministries. Yet evangelicals felt that the moral influence model was too optimistic about human potential and did not take sin, eternal life, and the spiritual realm seriously enough. To challenge these tendencies, evangelicals increasingly championed the substitutionary model as a "fundamental" of Christian faith. By the early twentieth-century, a "liberal-fundamentalist" controversy had emerged. These two models were so basic to each side that they seemed to be the only legitimate options.

But as World War II approached, the Swedish theologian Gustaf Aulen proposed that *Christus Victor* provided a third valid option.[5] Despite its prominence in Eastern Christianity, *Christus Victor* had long been neglected in the West, mainly because it seemed overly paradoxical (as we will see), and because it allotted a large role to oppressive, demonic powers. But as war's horrors engulfed the globe, the notion that superhuman malevolent powers might have a hand in it seemed increasingly plausible.

Over the last half century, Western theology's appreciation for *Christus Victor* has grown alongside increasing contacts with Eastern Christians. The moral influence model, whose views of evil and spiritual reality came to seem too shallow, has been largely neglected by ecumenical Protestants (who are, in many respects, the successors of Protestant liberals).[6] At the same time, evangelical Protestants have again become socially involved and interested in atonement models other than substitution, though many still consider it foundational.[7] Broadly speaking, ecumenical theologians are interested in atonement models with a sociopolitical side; evangelical theologians in models that incorporate personal and spiritual dimensions.

My empathy with both evangelical and ecumenical concerns has led me to explore *Christus Victor*. My own tradition, the Anabaptist-Mennonite, has always taken moral and social concerns seriously, but also stressed personal commitment and conversion and been strongly biblical.[8] However, we have seldom developed explicit theologies on traditional themes, including atonement. Consequently, as I approach Scripture, I feel free to draw on various models to help me understand and articulate its meaning theologically. Accordingly, although the Bible will provide the main source and sole norm of the theology below,[9] I will often draw on *Christus Victor* as found in Eastern Orthodoxy, especially in Irenaeus (ca. 135–ca. 202 CE). It will be developed in light of current ecumenical and evangelical concerns, particularly the issue of violence.

However, I cannot possibly construct a complete atonement theology from Scripture within this essay's limits. My main task, then, will be to present the paradigm that emerges from my work, shaped largely by *Christus Victor*, to show readers how particular passages and themes look from that perspective, and what new, perhaps unsuspected, meanings emerge. However, I will include many biblical texts in the footnotes for readers to examine for themselves.

Evil, Sin, and Judgment

Nonviolence is perhaps critiqued most often for failing to take evil seriously; for being too optimistic about human nature. The substitutionary model of atonement, in contrast, is often credited for its "realistic" appraisal of evil. This model displays some affinities with a certain sociopolitical outlook. God the Father is the ultimate governor of all societies. He must uphold justice, which is "subject to law," and cannot simply "forgive something that is disordered in His kingdom."[10] For God the Father, the smallest infraction of the law (divine law, at least) merits the harshest lethal penalty. Many people find this model supportive of governments that punish evil and seek to prevent its outbreak by vigorous violent measures.

The moral influence model, which highlights Jesus' teaching and example, has sometimes supported nonviolence; but while its nineteenth-century proponents appreciated evil's systemic nature,[11] they envisioned humankind overcoming this in an evolutionary advance toward God's kingdom, which today seems unrealistic. Moral influence theory's optimism and its preoccupation with the kingdom's earthly features seldom left room for power strong enough to truly counter evil.

If atonement theory is to deal realistically with evil and violence, must it incline toward substitution, as many evangelicals still suppose? Or might *Christus Victor* provide a plausible option? To decide, let us begin with its understanding of evil.

According to *Christus Victor,* Adam and Eve transgressed God's command. Substitutionary theory stresses this, and that it involved *disobedience* to God. *Christus Victor* highlights this also—but adds that disobedience involved *obedience* to another lord: the serpent. By submitting to this lord, Eve, Adam, and their descendants not only turned away from God, they also subjected themselves to the serpent's dominion. This finally resulted in death—but not simply because God decreed it as a legal penalty for disobedience. Submission to the serpent intrinsically led toward death because it cut people off from God, life's source. The Holy Spirit, the Spirit of life, who had originally dwelt close to Adam and Eve, withdrew, leaving a void in their hearts.[12]

91

Subjectively considered, this first sin was impelled by greed for more than God allotted our first parents, overwhelmingly abundant though this was. This sin therefore was robbery: snatching what belonged to another. It is hardly coincidental that the serpent suggested this act—the very act through which it bound humankind. For in so doing, the serpent itself was employing what Irenaeus called "violent means," for "it insatiably snatched away what was not its own," because humans "were by nature property of the omnipotent God."[13]

This greed swiftly spread through the void in human hearts left by the Spirit's departure. As humankind multiplied, greed inevitably fomented rivalry and jealousy. It is hardly coincidental that the next recorded sin was Cain's murder of Abel (Gen. 4:2-16). Before long, Lamech was boasting about avenging himself "seventy-sevenfold" (Gen. 4:23-24). The earth became so filled with corruption and violence that God destroyed most of it in a flood (Gen. 6:5-13).

In *Christus Victor*, then, sin is not only a human activity and disposition; it is chiefly bondage to sin, a suprahuman, quasi-personal power. Sin is a force that strives to snatch creatures away from God's order and subject them to its own rule, but thereby departs from life's source and, along with its captives, inevitably surges toward death. Sin, through this lust to possess and control, and the fears this arouses, binds people inwardly. Outwardly it spreads through corporate structures, twisting them into channels that spread and further magnify those lusts and fears and further intensify their distortive, violent force. This momentum spreads not only through general forces such as death, sin, and the flesh (e.g., Rom. 5, 6, 8), but also more specific agents with quasi-political and quasi-religious titles.[14]

What might this look like more concretely? A young person, agitated by fear of poverty and desire for pleasures, might devote his or her life to making money (mammon, in biblical terms).[15] Initial success might bring greater security, enjoyment, and status—but also arouse desires for more. Eventually, the necessity of making payments and moving further up the ladder to secure one's status and income could become all-consuming. It could erode that person's relationships, health, and emotional well-being. Competition with others would intensify; dishonesty and accumulation of power and its unfair use against others (violence) would become necessary to stay on top. This person would now be enmeshed in institutions and behaviors that had been chosen, yet whose collective momentum swept on, enslaving that person at the same time. These would increasingly sever one from God's life, and finally lead to eternal death.

To understand sin's operation from another angle, let us consider how Irenaeus perceived human nature as originally created. Western theology usually envisions Adam and Eve as mature immortal adults, fully appreciating the significance of God's command. Their disobedience, then, was a drastic "fall" from that height. But for Irenaeus, Eve and Adam were like children: mortal, yet designed to gradually acquire immortality as they journeyed through life and its tasks in response to God's Spirit.[16] Eastern Orthodoxy calls this process *divinization*. This may appear to mean actually becoming God, in essence. But divinization, rather, is transformation of our thoroughly human nature by divine energies.[17] This process sounds something like the moral influence notion of humanity evolving from primitive beginnings toward God's kingdom. Yet God's divinizing Spirit not only enters deeply into historical life, but also transcends it in a way difficult for that model to conceptualize.

According to Irenaeus, our childlike first parents did not so much reject a well-understood command directly as turn aside from it: by following another voice, taking another path. This notion has been criticized for minimizing sin's strength. But let us look more closely, for this notion, like others in *Christus Victor*, is paradoxical and has several sides.

First, it entails that humans are both responsible for, and victims of, sin. We go along with or commit ourselves to other lords—such as those life-styles and structures that enable us to acquire wealth or security and defend them against others. Yet humans are also victims of these lords, or life-styles and structures. For they intensify and distort our inward desires and fears, and urge and draw us onward with an outward collective momentum. Neither of these can we break by ourselves. These powers draw us into interconnected networks of sinful influences, structures, and oppressive entanglements. We suffer not only the direct consequences of our own acts, but also the assaults of these collective forces. Since these are directed toward domination and death, ever-widening injustice and violence spread in their wake. God holds us responsible for our allegiance to these lords. Yet the sufferings they inflict are often excessively cruel and arouse God's compassion.

This means, second, that God normally judges sin *indirectly*: by handing people over to the lords they choose. This implies, on one level, that these lords execute God's judgments. In this sense, these powers function as God's servants.[18] But on a deeper level they are God's enemies, whom God works to destroy. Said otherwise: God, on one level, allows other powers to punish sin, ultimately with eternal death. Yet on a deeper level God works to save those under their judgment.[19]

This notion of sin and judgment entails a third paradox: the powers' rule can be considered both just and unjust. The powers punish people justly because people choose them as their lords.[20] But on a deeper level, their rule is unjust. For it is rooted in a drive that violates God's rule and order by stealing away God's creatures and dominating them. This drive is violent because it robs not only God, but also creatures of their created destiny. This demonic drive would, if it could, separate all creatures from God's life, and thereby destroy them—and even God. Nothing could be more violent.

Several Comparisons

Before these paradoxes entangle us, let me briefly back up and compare *Christus Victor* with Western Christianity's two major atonement models. Whereas *Christus Victor* involves many paradoxes, the substitutionary and moral influence models can be stated much more simply—even as brief syllogisms, once one accepts their definitions of sin or moral goodness, respectively.[21] *Christus Victor*, however, is narrative in form. Its paradoxes arise partly from the way it traces the twists and turns of the biblical drama. Theological truth, as I understand it, cannot be satisfactorily expressed in general syllogisms, but is inseparable from the narrative in which Truth (the Son of God) embodied himself. This is one reason why I find *Christus Victor* more adequate on biblical grounds.

Further, the substitutionary model usually focuses on Jesus' *death* conceived as payment of sin's penalty, eternal death. Jesus' life is conceived as obedience that merits eternal life. It is these acts, conceived in these ways, which accomplish atonement. The specific content of Jesus' actions and teachings, strictly speaking, does not.

94

The moral influence model, in contrast, focuses mainly on Jesus' *life*, especially his specific acts and teachings, for they provide the pattern, inspiration, and awareness of divine love that draw us to, or at-one us with, God. Jesus' death heightened the impact of these factors.

Neither model ascribes distinct atoning significance to Jesus' *resurrection*. In substitution, atonement, strictly speaking, was completed with his death. Resurrection adds no more than do Jesus' specific acts and teachings, but provides evidence that atonement occurred. In moral influence, Jesus' resurrection simply extends the impact of his death, and thereby further extends the impact of his life.

In *Christus Victor*, contrastingly, Jesus' life, death, and resurrection each are essential, for they are acts in a drama. The first two by themselves could hardly provide at-one-ment. For, as we will see, they ended with his apparent defeat by the powers. If any act was primary, it was his *resurrection* victory.[22] However, *Christus Victor* is no tight syllogistic theory. It provides a narrative outline, or dramatic "plot," whose contents can vary somewhat in different formulations. My formulation, then, which follows, will incorporate several biblical themes that some versions of *Christus Victor* have not, and a few that appear in substitutionary and moral influence models.

Contemporary retrievals of *Christus Victor* often stress its *conflictive* dimension: Jesus' struggle with evil powers. If its Eastern Orthodox expressions are taken seriously, however, a *transformative* dimension must be included. I will sketch this first, then the conflictive dimension.

Christus Victor: Transformative Dimension

Irenaeus called this aspect of atonement *recapitulation*. Jesus walked the path that God originally set before Adam and Eve—the path that would lead all humans to their ultimate destiny.[23] Unlike our first parents, Jesus, the second Adam, continually obeyed God's commands (as stressed in the substitutionary model and assumed in the moral influence model). As he responded to the Spirit's guidance, his humanity was increasingly divinized. This process culminated with Jesus' bodily resurrection, through which he was fully divinized and became the first human to be entirely at-oned with God—the first fruits of many to follow. Jesus' specific actions and teachings were not simply instances of his general obedience, as in the substitutionary model. More like the moral influence model, *Christus Victor* considers every behavior that was necessary to Jesus' recapitulation of Adam and Eve's path essential to what at-one-ment with God *means:* to being the kind of person, for attaining the kind of salvation, which at-ones humans with God.[24]

As risen, Jesus now offers at-one-ment through participation with him, his Father, and his Spirit chiefly through incorporation into his body, the church. The Holy Spirit returns to the depths of the human heart, dispelling sin's greedy, fearful, violent inward rule. This inevitably transforms people's outward behavior and relationships in all spheres, including the sociopolitical.

Christus Victor: Conflictive Dimension

To recapitulate the human task, Jesus had to not only obey God but also resist the forces of evil as Adam and Eve had not, to avoid coming under their dominion. A struggle with demonic forces frames the synoptic Gospels. It centers on how Jesus would exercise his messianic role; on *precisely how* he would bring atonement, and therefore, on what atonement actually *is*. The messiah was most often expected to be a warrior who would conquer Rome militarily. Immediately after Jesus' baptism, which affirmed his messianic calling, Satan tempted him in the wilderness to exercise that calling in ways that would befit a glorious warrior. But Jesus resisted, adopting instead the suffering servant pattern.[25]

Jesus then began exorcising demons. When Israel's religious leaders opposed this, he replied that through these acts God's kingdom was defeating Satan's, but that these leaders, by opposing him, were joining forces with the latter (Matt. 12:24-30 and parallels). When Peter rejected the notion of a suffering messiah, Jesus attributed the suggestion to Satan (Matt. 16:21-23, Mark 8:31-33). Jesus, who was arousing increasing Roman and other opposition, could only have avoided suffering by becoming the expected warrior. Finally, at the cross, the crowds, Israel's religious leaders, and Roman soldiers again echoed the satanic, messianic temptation: If you are King of the Jews, prove it by saving yourself! (Matt. 27:39-44 and parallels). The Romans and the religious leaders had joined forces with Jesus' demonic opposition. These sociopolitical figures were the primary channels for, and primary agents of, those powers, though not wholly identical with them.

By continually resisting these powers and their recommended behaviors, Jesus remained under God's dominion. Rather than succumbing to another lord and being taken over by its violent greed to dominate others and their belongings, Jesus served others and was increasingly divinized by God's Spirit. *At the Gospels' heart,* then, we find a conflict over the basic means of bringing atonement: by war and domination, or by servanthood and the way of peace.[26]

Though theologians often declare this way impossible or unrealistic, Jesus clearly taught that it was not for him alone. It was to characterize all relationships in the kingdom he was bringing, as were his teachings on economic possessions and overcoming enmity among individuals and social groups.[27] These also reversed that insatiable grasping for wealth, status, and security loosed when Adam and Eve gave in to the devil's greed and violence. In other words, all these behaviors were intrinsic to Jesus' *recapitulation* of the human journey, which is the way of at-one-ment for everyone.

Nevertheless, Jesus' opposition to the powers apparently ended in defeat. But before showing how it led, instead, to his resurrection victory, let us compare *Christus Victor* with other models of the cross. Since atonement theories usually focus on Jesus' death, this discussion must be somewhat detailed. This detail, however, will illumine several distinctive features of *Christus Victor.*

Jesus' Death

Jesus' death certainly revealed God's love, as the moral influence model emphasizes. But reading the Bible in light of *Christus Victor* can help one see that this love was revealed preeminently in dying at the hands of, and for the sake of, God's enemies (see especially Rom. 5:10).

Substitutionists complain that moral influence overemphasizes God's love at the expense of God's justice. For God in that model apparently extends love and accepts us without demanding payment of sin's penalties from Jesus or anyone else. Substitutionary theory balances love and justice by aligning justice mainly with the Father's execution of the death penalty, and aligning love mainly with the Son's payment of it. Here God the Father, the ultimate governor of all societies, employs lethal violence. If *Christus Victor* is relevant to sociopolitical realities, it must also stress justice. Can it balance love and justice in another, nonviolent way?

In *Christus Victor* God exercises justice, in the main,[28] *indirectly:* by handing sinners over to the lords they choose. This procedure is just, for sinners subject themselves to those lords. God respects their choice and simply lets them go to follow their desire. The punishment fits the crime. Since everyone ultimately declares allegiance to powers that are under death's dominion, and that draw us into that dominion, God is just in finally letting us go, handing us over to death. God's final judgment does not so much inflict something as abandon us to the death we choose—or allow us to cut ourselves off from life's source. This kind of justice is nonviolent. Violence is coercive and deprives its victims of freedom. This justice respects our freedom and lets us follow the course we choose.

Were Jesus to share our fate, including the punishment we deserve, the death penalty would be executed, *directly,* by the powers ruling our world (by those operating, in Jesus' case, through religion and the violent state). Jesus bore *their* wrath, *not* his Father's, *directly.* To be sure, since the Father used these agents to execute justice, Jesus bore God's general judgment against sin, as we all do, *indirectly.* God continued to govern the universe, as the substitutionary model insists God must. Since final judgment is abandonment to death, which separates sinners from life's source, Jesus experienced that final abandonment to death and hell awaiting all who abandon God. His final cry, "My God, my God, why have you forsaken me?" (Matt. 27:45-50; Mark 15:33-37) hardly makes sense otherwise.

But still, one could ask, was this judgment really just? For Jesus never abandoned his Father. Was his Father just, then, in abandoning him? Jesus never deserved this penalty of sin. Was it just, then, to have him pay it?

My response begins by insisting that relationships between the Father and Son be explained chiefly in terms of love. The New Testament portrays them deeply united throughout Jesus' life and after his resurrection. We should not suppose that they became divided and hostile on the cross without very good reasons.

The question above envisions Father and Son set over against each other, perhaps with the Father "up above," demanding or inflicting a penalty, and the Son "down below," painfully paying it. Taken to an extreme, this picture can look like and even legitimate child abuse.[29] To be sure, Jesus obeyed his Father all the way to the cross. Yet this was entirely voluntary. Closely examined, the Gospels provide a broad narrative portrait of God—Father, Son, and Spirit—working cooperatively to bring humans, who have become estranged and captive to alien powers, back to themselves.[30]

This God does not simply reestablish outward, formal connections. God enters deeply into the human situation, to draw people from within their hearts and their everyday existence into communion with Godself and one another. This begins when the Son, as the second Adam, fully shares our human situation,[31] and by walking Adam's path in communion with the Spirit and Father, brings his full human reality into divinizing communion with them. This process continues, after his resurrection, as God's Spirit draws other people into this communion.

Divine love, as revealed in this biblical narrative, is servantlike, self-giving, and self-sacrificing (as in the moral influence model). Now let us again consider the justice of Jesus' death. Let us ask: What would happen if someone living wholly by this love entered a hostile territory ruled by violence and domination? What if he sought to express this love toward its inhabitants, who were his enemies? It seems inevitable that he would suffer. Indeed, if this territory were ultimately ruled by death, whose deepest impulse is to destroy the life from which that love flows, death would eventually attack that person. If he kept on living by self-giving, nonviolent love, death's antithesis, that person would finally be killed. (This is why Jesus "had to die"; because God's love operates this way in the face of evil, not because some general, abstract law dictates it.)[32]

In this biblical narrative, however, the Father and the Holy Spirit accompany and strengthen the Son on this journey. Accordingly, the picture of the cross sketched above changes. No longer is the Father opposed to or "above" the Son (and the Spirit omitted). Instead, the evil powers are on one side, and God—Father, Son, and Spirit—on the other. God the Father and Spirit, indeed, let the Son die—yet not simply to pay a penalty, but because this is the inevitable outcome of their mission of love in a hostile world. It is the powers, ranged over against God, who inflict the death penalty *although Jesus was innocent*. God does not inflict such a penalty, save in the *indirect* sense of allowing it to be exacted, without intervening violently to prevent it, because this was an inevitable consequence of their mission of self-sacrificing love.

Therefore, it *was* unjust for Jesus to pay a penalty he did not deserve; yet *not* because God demands such penalties—but because the powers of evil do. The powers' violent way of domination and death strives to subject and ultimately destroy everyone and everything, whether they deserve it or not.

This narrative portrait, moreover, positions the powers over against not only Jesus, but the entire Godhead. Not only are his Father and Spirit not agents of violent punishment, they, too, suffer under it. How is this possible?

Jürgen Moltmann points out that people suffer from death in two main ways. One is through actually dying. Each person undergoes this once (though near-death experiences can include some such suffering). The second way is grieving as a loved one dies. Most people experience this more than once, and some people many times. At the cross, then, it is not only Jesus who undergoes the pain of dying. The Father grieves deeply at Jesus' pain, and the loss of his beloved Son. The cross reveals not only the Son's love for us, but also the Father's love for us and his Son.[33] Yet Jesus, who shared the human situation fully, experienced that awful final abandonment by God (Matt. 27:45-50, Mark 15:33-37). Could this really have resulted from his Father's grieving love?

It could, I propose, if the Father's love, like his, were nonviolent. If both Father and Son undertook the mission of self-giving love into a hostile world, then both arrived at the same painful self-sacrifice and neither would intervene in that situation violently. When the powers grasped Jesus, he refused to grasp any violent means of protection (Matt. 26:47-53 and parallels). Likewise, his Father refused to counter the powers violently, but simply let Jesus go, with the result that Jesus was engulfed by their violence and its ultimate expression, death. The Father, then, "delivered over" his Son—but only out of grief and self-sacrificing love that refused to employ violence.[34] This, rather than any punishment inflicted by his Father, is why Jesus experienced death as those imprisoned by the powers do: abandonment by God.

But did the Son's love for the Father then fail? On the contrary, it was precisely this love that enabled Jesus to enter and endure this hellish experience. How? Recall that the Holy Spirit also suffered under the powers. It was "through the eternal Spirit" that Jesus "offered himself without blemish to God" (Heb. 9:14). At this point of their deepest separation, then, the Father and Son were still united by the Spirit of love, flowing back and forth between them. The divine unity of purpose, character, and love prevailed, even though Jesus experienced abandonment's horror as humans do.[35]

This meant, further, that God, the entire divine reality, in different ways as Father, Son, and Spirit, entered into death. This entailed, moreover, as Moltmann beautifully says:

> All human history...is taken up into this "history of God."...There is no suffering which in this history of God is not God's suffering; no death which has not been God's death in the history upon Golgotha. Therefore there is no life, no fortune and no joy which have not been integrated by his history into the eternal life, the eternal joy of God.[36]

Not every version of *Christus Victor* includes all this. Still, the theology I am developing understands atonement's core as this model does. At-one-ment occurs, at bottom, through *participation*: God's own participation in our life and death through Jesus' history, which enables humans, and ultimately other creatures, to participate in God's life (in God's *energies*, not God's *essence*).[37]

Earlier, I called this participatory aspect of *Christus Victor* its *transformative* dimension. This transformation does not occur, of course, unless our bondage to hostile powers is broken. I included Jesus' struggle with them in this model's *conflictive* dimension. Let us revisit the *conflictive* dimension by returning to the historical drama.

Jesus' Resurrection

Most versions of *Christus Victor* apply legal concepts to Jesus' life only in a marginal way. Yet legal concepts become central in all versions of *Christus Victor* when they consider the contrast between Jesus' crucifixion and resurrection. In explaining this, they draw on broad biblical themes such as God's righteousness and justice far more often than specific concepts such as verdict or payment. These broad themes must be understood as processes or in narrative fashion, like God's "judgment," which I recently described as the process of letting people reap the consequences of their choices.

Within the biblical narrative, Jesus' execution *meant* that he and his claims to bring God's peaceable kingdom were false, and that his enemies were in the right. The cross apparently confirmed his religious and political opponents' claims to be the true guarantors of peace—insofar as this was "realistically" possible on earth (cf. Luke 22:25). What did it mean, then, when Jesus, who was condemned as a false prophet and political rebel, was raised as God's true Messiah and Prince of Peace? When the one rejected by his fellow humans was raised as the first to attain human destiny?

In biblical terms, this meant that the apparent verdict of the cross was reversed. Suddenly, the powers that crucified Jesus were identified as God's opponents—as agents of apostasy, oppression, and violence—not of fidelity, justice, and peace, as they pretended. The multitudes, who had gone along, actively or passively, with these powers, were also shown to be God's enemies.[38] For God the Father, who had refrained from violent intervention in his Son's death, now intervened through his resurrecting Spirit to bring justice. Christ was now "Victor" over the powers, judging them at the apex of their violent drive to subject all creatures to their dominion, and to exterminate even God. Was God, finally, vengeful and violent?

On the contrary, God judged the powers in the same way as humans. God simply let them pursue their chosen path to its end. Left to their own murderous devices, they inevitably executed the one who opposed them. *Christus Victor* theories explain the resurrection verdict, more precisely, from three main angles.

First, some explain it in precise legal terms. Since sinners subject themselves to the devil's lordship, it is sometimes said that Satan had the "right" to imprison and punish them all. Since God allowed this process to proceed, it could be said that God entrusted the devil and the demonic cohorts with this task. However, Jesus never subjected himself to Satan. Satan, consequently, had no right to execute him. By that act, then, the devil violated, or overstepped the boundaries of, lawful jurisdiction. The resurrection, from this legal angle, disqualified the devil and installed Jesus as ruler of humankind.

Not all proponents of *Christus Victor*, however, accept this legal explanation. Since patristic times some have objected that the devil, who had sought ever since Eden to rob humans from God and murder them, had no such "right."[39] This suggests that in *Christus Victor* the powers' rule can be considered lawful, if at all, only in the paradoxical sense that God allows it for a time, even though it is lawless in the deeper sense.

Jesus' resurrection, second, also judged the powers by revealing how oppressive and unjust they were. The resurrection cast its light back on Jesus' struggle with them during his life and death. The contrast between sinful humankind's misery under their rule and the way of life that Jesus taught and offered became graphically clear. Central to this contrast, we have seen, was the opposition between their violence and his nonviolent, peaceful way.

Finally, biblical justice involves more than a sentence that penalizes the guilty and rewards the righteous, even when it graphically reveals the contrast between them. Biblical justice also sets wrong situations right. It destroys the operations of evil forces and establishes the forces of good.[40] In *Christus Victor*, the resurrection "verdict" consisted, above all, in the return of the Spirit of life, whom humankind since Adam had rejected, with strength to enliven even the dead. God's Spirit began dissolving the possessive lusts and demonic fears of many hearts with gentle, but powerful, servantlike love.

Christ, through his Spirit, now breaks repeatedly into Satan's forfeited kingdom, reuniting humans and other creatures with God and one another. Especially through the church, Jesus draws people into his own communion with his Father and Spirit. Here again, at-one-ment is basically *transformative*, or participatory. Yet its continuation, like its origins, has a *conflictive* side. Jesus' followers continue to struggle with opposing powers.[41] But since those who participate in atonement follow the pattern provided by Jesus' life, his Spirit works through the same self-giving, and if need be suffering, love.

In none of these three ways was Jesus' resurrection "verdict," or his continuing conquest of the powers, violent. To be sure, a notion of Jesus the Victor or conqueror has sometimes been used to justify violence. This usually happens when the risen Jesus is divorced from his earthly journey and reimaged as a military hero. Such distortions are possible only by ignoring *how* Jesus conquered—precisely by rejecting the warrior messiah image and responding to violence nonviolently.

Final Comparisons

At first glance *Christus Victor*, as I have developed it, may appear quite similar to the moral influence model. In both models Jesus does not simply at-one individuals in a spiritual sense, but draws them into new relationships with God, one another, and other creatures. These relationships, or God's kingdom, are shaped by behaviors that express God's love. Jesus' saving work involves teaching and exemplifying these behaviors along with their transforming impact on people. By following this way unflinchingly to death, Jesus magnified the impact, or revelation, of God's love and kingdom. Some versions of moral influence include nonviolence among Jesus' main teachings.

Moral influence, at least in Protestant liberal versions, and *Christus Victor*, in Eastern Christianity and especially Irenaeus, differ mainly in their explanatory categories. The former tends to explain atonement in terms of historical forces, conceived as moral, social, and physical processes (*historicism*). In the latter, divine and evil powers transcend the historical matrix. Though they operate through human individuals and institutions, they cannot be equated with or reduced to these.[42] *Christus Victor*, then, reinforces twentieth-century criticisms of moral influence: it cannot take evil's destructive power seriously enough. Neither are its spiritual resources strong enough to combat evil in its depths, not simply in its surface manifestations. If *Christus Victor* is consistently demythologized, as it sometimes is today, distinctions between it and the moral influence model can be blurred. Nonviolence can be reduced to human moral effort guided by an inspiring example.

What about "substitution"? This term could perhaps describe Jesus' work in the sense that he attained something for us that we could not attain for ourselves on which we can rely instead of on our own inadequacies. Yet substituting can imply that one thing (what Jesus did) wholly replaces something very different (what we do or should do). This is possible when the replacement is conceived as a thing that can be transferred, like a payment or legal verdict, to a person's account without intrinsically changing that person. Such concepts can lead people to suppose that because Jesus suffered, we do not have to; because Jesus obeyed

God, we do not need to. This can divorce atonement from following him, including his nonviolent way.

But let us consider: How is Jesus' death, for example, "transferred" to us? How does it benefit us? By exempting us from physical death? Hardly. By providing a free pass around hell and into heaven? Such a notion, even if remotely accurate, trivializes what he suffered and what we suffer. I would stress that Jesus passed through death, which is abandonment by God, which we all deserve, *alone*—and that consequently we need not. Why? Basically because when we pass through death, we will not be alone, for he will be with us.

This "benefit," like all others in *Christus Victor*, is available only through Jesus' resurrection. It is available because his Father and Spirit accompanied Jesus through death, whose grief and pain could not destroy the Godhead's mutually self-expending love, which raised Jesus again to life. Consequently, when people in communion with Jesus pass through death, he will *accompany* them. He who passed through these terrors alone will be with us in our terrors; his Father and Spirit, who experienced death's grief, will be with us in our grief. Together they will usher us into resurrection life.

Jesus' death, then, did something *for us,* and also *before* us and *outside* of us, which he gives *to us*—as substitutionary theory insists. Yet we receive that benefit chiefly by *participation* in Christ—when the risen Jesus shares it with us, incorporates us into it, better, into *himself*, with his Father through his Spirit. Nevertheless, participation language, by itself, can blur distinctions between participants. It can blur the otherness of Jesus and his work, and thereby its character as gift, as grace. Substitutionary concepts can accent a contrasting objectivity. I do not find terms such as *transfer of payment* or *legal right* by themselves well suited to express atonement's participatory dynamism. Yet terms like these appear in Scripture. They have been used, and still can be used, in a secondary sense in *Christus Victor*.

Practical Significance

Given *Christus Victor*'s complexities, readers might well ask: Is it simply an intellectual construct? Or can it actually help us deal with escalating violence today? I propose that when one's theology is informed by and informs a spiritual and ethical life of increasing love for God and others, and a deepening sensitivity to evil and suffering, this model can sharpen our focus and guide our actions in the following ways:

1. By expanding "atonement" into a useful framework for appraising all kinds of divisions and conflicts, and all efforts toward overcoming them. Atonement is relevant not only to personal and spiritual salvation, but also to every way in which creatures and God move toward unity, and to every obstacle that divides them.

2. By enabling us to perceive violence as not simply one kind of sin, but central and related to all forms of sin; and to perceive the relevance of nonviolence to healing and wholeness of every sort. This will increase our sensitivities to the role of violence in any situation and stimulate our imaginations to find nonviolent ways of dealing with it.

3. Nonviolence, when rooted in Jesus' overall work, will be neither passive nor escapist in face of conflict, but a courageous response to it. The self-giving love that energizes it will draw Christians, like their Lord, into the midst of everyday life and its sufferings. "Nonviolence," which only expresses what one does not do, probably does not best denote this behavior; nor even does "nonviolent resistance," for it still accents negative over positive action.

4. Nonviolence will be seen in light of the already dawning kingdom that Jesus brought and brings. Jesus' commands will become not so much specific instructions as imperatives, when one is threatened by violence, to respond in better, more creative ways—because God's kingdom is at hand![43] Perhaps the best short description of what I mean by nonviolence is: "Do not repay anyone evil for evil ... but overcome evil with good" (Rom. 12:17, 21).

5. Guided by their kingdom vision and God's creative Spirit, Christians and churches can respond to violent situations by developing alternative structures and behaviors that reflect the inward and outward transformations that atonement brings (e.g., interracial schools and economic ventures in situations of interracial violence and strife).

6. Nevertheless, God still entrusts government to institutions that employ violence, and these still promote some degree of civil order and good.

Nonviolent Christians can work with these insofar as they pursue such aims. Since atonement enhances all aspects of life as God intends it, Christians can support all efforts that further this and allow them to live wholly by Jesus' way. However, Christians must be careful not to identify, implicitly or explicitly, any social or political effort with God's. Whenever possible, they should guide these toward further approximation of God's kingdom.

Notes

1. For a good example, see C. S. Lewis, "Why I Am Not a Pacifist" in *The Weight of Glory* (New York: Simon & Schuster, 1996), 53-71. Most of the teachings considered are in Jesus' "Sermon on the Mount" (Matt. 5–7), especially turning the other cheek, giving an adversary one's cloak and one's coat, and going the second mile (6:38-42).

2. *Christus Victor* also expands atonement's significance to include the whole creation, but because of space limitations, I cannot include its environmental implications.

3. In Anselm's *Cur Deus Homo*, trans. and ed. by Jasper Hopkins and Herbert Richardson as *Why God Became Man* in *Anselm of Canterbury*, vol. 3 (New York: Edwin Mellen, 1975), 49-137.

4. Among its main exponents were Horace Bushnell, *The Vicarious Sacrifice*, 2 vols. (New York: Scribner's, 1903 [originally published in 1877]); Albrecht Ritschl, *The Christian Doctrine of Justification and Reconciliation*, vol. III (Clifton, NJ: Reference Book Publishers, 1966 [originally published in 1874]; Hastings Rashdall, *The Idea of Atonement in Christian Theology* (London: Macmillan, 1919).

5. Gustaf Aulen, *Christus Victor* (New York: Macmillan, 1960 [originally published in 1930]).

6. In 1948 the larger Protestant bodies (Presbyterian, Methodist, Lutheran, Episcopal, and so forth) joined with the Eastern Orthodox to form the World Council of Churches. Whereas the liberal tendencies of most Protestant members have often clashed with the more conservative Orthodox outlook, mutual interests and positive links between Orthodox and evangelicals have surfaced over the last quarter century.

7. This is perhaps most evident in "The Gospel of Jesus Christ: An Evangelical Celebration," published by the largest evangelical publication *Christianity Today* 43, no. 7 (June 14, 1999), especially "Affirmations and Denials," #8 and #9.

8. Since Mennonites have often been somewhat isolated from society, their concerns might better be called "communal," which have lately become more broadly "social." Some might say that the morally serious, ethnically ingrown Mennonites stressed "commitment" *rather than* "conversion." But I find "conversion" accurate also, though usually less dramatic than the evangelical kind.

9. Theologians reflect on material from many *sources*: Though Scripture should be primary, hymns, liturgies, personal and corporate experiences, historical events, and many others play important roles. Scripture, however, provides the only *norm* for assessing the truth of theological affirmations.

10. *Cur Deus Homo*, 68-69; therefore God cannot "forgive sin out of mercy alone, apart from any repayment of the honor stolen from him" (68).

11. Bushnell, *Vicarious Sacrifice*, especially vol. I, especially 255-74; Ritschl, *Christian Doctrine of Justification*, especially 334-50.

12. Irenaeus, *Against Heresies*, in Alexander Robers and James Donaldson, eds., *The Ante-Nicene Fathers*, vol. I (Grand Rapids, MI: Eerdmans, 1979 [reprint]), 313-567; 5:21.2-3 , 23.1-2, 31.3, 32. Biblically, the Spirit's withdrawal is inferred from the dramatic difference in humankind's relationship to God made by the Spirit's outpouring as a direct consequence of Jesus' saving work (especially Acts 2; 10:44-48; John 16:7-15; Gal. 4:3-7; Eph. 1:13-14). Although not entirely absent from human life before this, the Spirit's presence was more sporadic.

13. Irenaeus, *Against Heresies*, 5:1.1; cf. James 4:1-3.

14. "Thrones (*thronoi*)," "dominions (*kuriotētes*)," "principalities (*archai*)," and "powers (*exousiai*)" appear in Colossians 1:16. *Archai, exousiai* and *kuriotētes*, along with *dunameis* (also translated "powers") are found in Ephesians 4:21. *Archai* could designate political rulers and was related to *archōn*, or "prince," as in "prince of this world" (John 12:31; 14:30; 16:11). *Exousiai* and *thronoi* could also denote earthly rulers, and *kuriotēs* earthly authority. *Archai* and *exousiai* appear together in Ephesians 3:10; 6:12; Colossians 2:10; 15; and Titus 3:1; and both appear with *dunameis* in 1 Corinthians 15:24. *Dunameis* is also found with *archai* in Romans 8:38, with *exousiai* in 1 Peter 3:22, and alone in Matthew 24:29 and parallels. *Dunameis, thronos*, and *exousia* occur together in Revelation 13:2. "Elemental spirits (*stoicheia*)" were religious entities with a somewhat political flavor (Gal. 4:3, 9; Col. 2:8, 20).

15. Jesus called God and mammon "masters," both of which no one can possibly serve (Matt. 6:24; Luke 16:27). His general critique of wealth often involved this opposition (e.g., Matt. 6:19-21).

16. Irenaeus, *Against Heresies*, 2:28.1; 3:20.1-2, 23.5; 4:38.4, 39.2. Biblical support is found in the notion that humans, as created, are oriented toward God's call (see my *Self, Earth and Society* [Downers Grove, IL: InterVarsity Press, 1997], 262-69).

17. The *essence-energies* distinction was formulated by Gregory Palamas (1296–1359). Many Orthodox, however, trace this general notion much further back, sometimes to Irenaeus (cf. *Against Heresies*, 3:24.2). Biblically, divinization by God's direct touch, or energies, is affirmed especially by the Holy Spirit's indwelling; by many references to being, or abiding, "in" Christ and/or his Spirit and Father; and the "new birth." (See my *A Contemporary Anabaptist Theology: Biblical, Historical, Constructive* [Downers Grove, IL: InterVarsity Press, 2004], chapter 5).

18. Although the punishment that they inflict is God's only in an *indirect* sense, it is no less severe and no less serious a response to evil than direct punishment from God. For judgments in this life involve further subjection to death's power and result, for those who never repent, in complete subjugation to death and separation from God after they die.

19. A major biblical support for this notion of sin and judgment is its predominance in the Old Testament. As capsulized in Judges 2:13-18, Israel "abandoned the LORD, and worshiped" neighboring gods like "Baal and the Astartes." Consequently, Yahweh handed them over, or "sold them into the power of their enemies all around." Nevertheless, "the LORD would be moved to pity by their groaning because of those who ... oppressed them." And so God "delivered them from the hand of their enemies" by raising up Judges. Though Yahweh often declares that "I" will punish Israel, this is nearly always carried out by other nations.

20. This is why, according to Romans 13:1-2, God has subordered (*tetagmenai, diatagē*) the governing authorities (*exousiai*, the common word for "evil powers") to the divine purposes, but not "instituted" them in the direct sense, as many translations imply. In the view I am developing, governments function much as those that represented the gods of the nations in the Old Testament (cf. my *Christian Theology: An Eschatological Approach*, vol. II [Scottdale, PA: Herald, 1989], 84-88, 147-54, cf. 82-84). Christ dismantled their final rule over humans by destroying the *reign* of death that they served (cf. Heb. 2:14-15), though neither death's *reality* nor theirs is yet fully destroyed (cf. 1 Cor. 15:25-28, 54-56; cf. note 43 below).

21. If one assumes that (1) fulfillment or infraction of a law brings salvation or damnation, and (2) all humans fail to fulfill this law and incur its penalty, it seems obvious that (3) for salvation to be possible, someone else must fulfill the law and pay the penalty. Anselm sought to show further, by reason and without reference to Scripture, how this entailed that God became human (*Cur Deus Homo*, 137). If one assumes with Bushnell that (1) God is love, and (2) love is "essentially vicarious in its own nature, identifying the subject with others, and taking on itself the burden of their evils" (*Vicarious Sacrifice* vol. I, 42), and (3) love "works only by inducement; that is, by impressions, or attractions" (403), the main themes of moral influence theory seem obvious. Both models, of course, exist in various versions, and include features that cannot be deduced so obviously.

22. Here is a reason for preferring *Christus Victor* on biblical grounds: It incorporates those phases essential to the atonement narrative, whereas the other models omit or seriously misconstrue at least one (resurrection).

23. Irenaeus, *Against Heresies*, 2:24.4; 3:16.6, 18.7, 19.1-3, 20.2, 21.10–22.1, 22.3-4. The second Adam motif is strong in Philippians 2:6-11, Romans 5:12-21, and 1 Corinthians 15:20-23, 45-49. Jesus' "obedience," central to this motif in Philippians 2:8 and Romans 5:19, also appears in Hebrews 5:8 where he most clearly pioneered the path intended for all people (Hebrews 2:10-18; 3:14; 4:14-16; 5:7-10; 6:19-20; 12:1-4; *archēgos* ["leader" or "pioneer"] occurs in Hebrews 2:10; 12:2; and also Acts 3:15; 5:31).

24. This is not expressed so unequivocally by every version of *Christus Victor*. Again, my claim is that this and my other major points are taught in Scripture, and that *Christus Victor* can help us grasp them more clearly.

25. For this and what follows see John Howard Yoder, *The Politics of Jesus* (Grand Rapids, MI: Eerdmans, 1972), 26-41; Oscar Cullmann, *Jesus and the Revolutionaries* (New York: Harper & Row, 1970); N. T. Wright, *Jesus and the Victory of God* (Minneapolis: Fortress Press, 1996), especially 477-539; cf. 274-319, 446-74, 651-53.

26. John records a similar struggle between Jesus and the prince of this world (John 12:31; 14:30; 16:11), though the centrality of violence is not as clear, save at points like John 15:12-13; 18:36. The Johannine writings highlight the struggle with demonic opposition in terms such as darkness, death, "the world," and various terms for the devil.

27. Jesus' promotion of peace over violence was integrally related to the reversals of contemporary social status that his kingdom entailed: of the rich over the poor, men over women, Jew over gentile, and the holy or "righteous" over the "sinners" or profane (see Finger, *Self, Earth and Society*, 337-41 and my *Christian Theology: An Eschatological Approach*, vol. I [Scottdale, PA: Herald, 1985], 282-91).

28. I do not think a biblically based theology can assert, unequivocally, that God *never* punishes directly. This may have happened with particular persons in particular circumstances (e.g., Uzzah in 2 Sam. 6:6-11). In my view, equivalent punishment (an eye for an

eye, and so forth) is just in a certain sense, though it must often be enacted coercively. God would be just in inflicting such penalties directly. When God avoids this, it is not because God could not do it. Instead, God's usual indirect process flows from restraint or patience or desire to rule through a form of justice that respects creaturely freedom.

29. For a helpful discussion, see Darby Kathleen Ray, *Deceiving the Devil: Atonement, Abuse, and Ransom* (Cleveland: Pilgrim Press, 1998).

30. See Jürgen Moltmann, *The Trinity and the Kingdom* (San Fransisco: Harper & Row, 1981), 61-96; Finger, *Christian Theology*, 434-38.

31. His birth is attributed to the Holy Spirit (Matt. 1:18, 20; Luke 1:35) from the Father (the Most High [Luke 1:35], the Mighty One [1:49], and so forth). At his baptism the Spirit descends and his Father commissions him (Matt. 3:16-17 and parallels).

32. Luke stresses this most (Luke 9:22; 17:25; 22:21, 37; 24:7, 26, 44; Acts 4:28; 17:3), but as a feature of God's saving historical activity (cf. Luke 2:49; 4:43; 13:33; 21:9, 37; Acts 1:16, 21; 3:21; 13:46; 23:11; 27:24).

33. Especially Romans 8:31-32 and 1 John 4:9-10; see Jürgen Moltmann, *The Crucified God* (New York: Harper & Row, 1974), 235-49; Moltmann, *Trinity and the Kingdom*, 75-83.

34. New Testament usage of *paradidōmi*, the standard term for "delivering over" to prison, torture, and death, indicates very clearly how judgment can be ascribed to God, but is directly exercised by others. *Paradidōmi* describes the Father only once, precisely in this self-expending, loving act (Rom. 8:32); but it often describes Judas's betrayal of Jesus to Israel's religious leaders, their handing him over to the Romans (e.g., Matt. 17:22; 20:18-19; 26:2; 26:15–27:18 and parallels; Acts 3:13), and Pilate's passing him on to executioners (e.g., Matt. 27:26 and parallels). People can be delivered over to Satan (1 Cor. 5:5; 1 Tim. 1:20), to whom all kingdoms have been delivered and who hands these kingdoms on to others (Luke 4:6). God punished humankind by delivering them over to what they desired (Rom. 1:24, 26, 28), and when Israel turned away from Yahweh to other gods, God turned away and delivered them over to the host of heaven (Acts 7:39-43).

35. "[O]n the cross the Father and the Son are so deeply separated that their relationship breaks off.... Yet on the cross [they] are at the same time so much one that they represent a single surrendering movement.... The surrender through the Father and the offering of the Son take place 'through the Spirit.' The Holy Spirit is therefore the link in the separation" (Moltmann, *Trinity and the Kingdom*, 82).

36. Moltmann, *The Crucified God*, 246.

37. Atonement, in all three major models, consists in the communication of something accomplished during Jesus' life, death, and resurrection to us. In substitution, these accomplishments become available mainly as payments or legal decisions that can be transferred to or reckoned to us judicially. Actual participation in or *impartation* of Jesus' life and death themselves follows as a consequence. Atonement itself tends to be judicial *imputation* of these. In the moral influence model, Jesus' life and death become available mainly through impacts or influences that they transmit, first to his disciples, and then down the generations through the lives of subsequent followers and the Bible. Though the Holy Spirit may aid this transmission, recipients do not participate in the risen Jesus as in *Christus Victor*.

38. I find this clearest in "justification" language, especially in Romans 3, though Western theology usually reduces justification to its spiritual and individual dimensions. In Romans, God's righteousness is publicly manifested through Jesus' history (3:21, 25-

26), showing that God alone is righteous, faithful, and true, and all humans unrighteous, faithless, and liars (3:4-5, cf. 19; see Finger, *Christian Theology*, 174-79, 184-87, and the sources cited; A. Katherine Grieb, *The Story of Romans* [Louisville: Westminster John Knox, 2002], 35-42). Since all people are bound together in sin (Rom. 1:18–2:29; 3:9-19, 23), no one group is uniquely responsible for Jesus' death—certainly not Jews. Rather, we are all condemned by his death as God's enemies. This can be explained within a moral influence framework (except for the deeper demonic dynamics): "We are linked in a solidarity of evil and guilt with all who have done the same before us, and all who will do the same after us. In so far then as we, by our conscious actions or passive consent, have repeated the sins which killed Jesus, we have made ourselves guilty of his death. If those who actually killed him stood before us, we ... would have to range ourselves with them as men of their own kind" (Walter Rauschenbusch, *A Theology for the Social Gospel* [New York: Macmillan, 1917], 259).

39. Aulen, *Christus Victor*, 47-55.

40. This is very evident in the Old Testament word for "righteousness," *tsedeqah*, although Western theologians have often understood its New Testament equivalent, *dikaiosunē*, as "legal justice" (stressed by the Romans) or "ethically" (stressed by the Greeks). With many recent theologians, I find that New Testament *dikaiosunē*, and hence "justification," carries this broader, even cosmic meaning (cf. note 39 above). This is the kind of justice involved in Jesus' resurrection. The Old Testament word for "justice," *mishpat*, often had a somewhat narrower, more specifically legal scope (see Norman Snaith, *Distinctive Ideas of the Old Testament* [New York: Schocken, 1964], 68-77).

41 Jesus destroyed death's *reign*, its capacity to sever us finally from God, and that of powers in its service to lead or subject us to death (Rom. 5:12-21; 6:5-14; 7:4–8:1, 12-17, 38-39; Heb. 2:14-15). Only his return, however, will destroy their active *reality* (1 Cor. 15:25-28, 54-56; Rev. 20:14).

42. Admittedly, these forces were often spiritualized in Eastern tradition, distancing religious from sociopolitical life. This error is the opposite of historicist reduction.

43. For instance, carrying the gear of a Roman soldier, Israel's enemy, a second mile was a creative response to oppression. Jesus was rejecting "militaristic nationalism" and "offering a different way of liberation ... which affirmed the humanness of the national enemy" and also "the destiny of Israel as the bringer of light to the world, not as the one who would crush the world with military zeal" (Wright, *Jesus and the Victory of God*, 450).

RESPONSES TO
THOMAS FINGER

Response to Thomas Finger
J. Denny Weaver

Affirmations

It should come as no surprise that I fully support Thomas Finger's conclusions that *Christus Victor* is a nonviolent atonement motif, and that it is the best atonement image for the modern world. I agree with his efforts to base *Christus Victor* in the narrative of Jesus, and with his effort to pose *Christus Victor* as an atonement motif with clear ethical implications for Christians living today in a violent world.

Points of Conversation

Although I agree with Finger's conclusion, I depart from his methodology. A few comments on methodology will then point to some differences between his version of *Christus Victor* and what I call narrative *Christus Victor*.

Finger's use of a church father lends credibility to this motif. Finger takes the motif of *Christus Victor* from Irenaeus, including the element of recapitulation, and then fills that image out with biblical materials, primarily but not exclusively from Genesis and from the Gospels. My own formulation, narrative *Christus Victor*, is anchored in the book of Revelation and the Gospels. The order of Revelation and then the Gospels is not mandatory for understanding the motif, but this presentation reflects the way in which I first began to articulate a rudimentary version of narrative *Christus Victor* many years ago. Gustaf Aulen's *Christus Victor* introduced me to the motif of *Christus Victor*. Although Aulen does not deal with Revelation, his articulation of the motif enabled me to discover it in Revelation and then to begin to narrate the life, death, and resurrection of Jesus in terms of the motif.

This contrast in the location of the beginning articulation of the motif—Irenaeus versus Revelation—points to what I suggest is the most basic difference between the way Finger and I each develop a *Christus*

Victor motif. Finger's basic methodology is synthesis, as can be easily observed from reading his earlier *Christian Theology: An Eschatological Approach* as well as his more recent book *A Contemporary Anabaptist Theology*. It appears that he sees all of doctrinal history as a seemingly flat or equally accessible repository of material on which to draw to construct his own view, and his intent is to synthesize as much as possible from this history into his own construction. In this case he chose Irenaeus as the source of an outline to fill out with biblical material. This view of the history of doctrine means that even as he states that *Christus Victor* "can better articulate the biblical materials," he draws on material from the other motifs to fill out and expand *Christus Victor*. This flat view of doctrinal history precludes observations such as linking the view of *Christus Victor* in Revelation to the ecclesiological stance of the early church and satisfaction and substitution motifs more clearly to the ecclesiology after the synthesis symbolized by Constantine and Theodosius. Rather, all these motifs are treated as free-floating entities from which one can take individual components at will. Examples are Finger's moves to retain the concept of punishment in *Christus Victor*, an impulse from substitutionary atonement, while mitigating it by explaining that God's punishment is indirect, and his redefinition of the concept of "substitution" itself. Thus he ends with a synthetic *Christus Victor* that also displays elements of substitution and moral influence atonement images.

My approach, which begins with Revelation and then moves to the Gospels, is less beholden to the specifics of the history of doctrine. Although narrative *Christus Victor* is clearly recognizable as *Christus Victor*, it is a new version of the motif not found elsewhere in this form. This beginning point in the biblical material, rather than a church father, emphasizes that every formulation of doctrine is a particular construct, which in turn makes clear that we are free to rethink and critique these received formulas rather than being obligated to accept them from an authoritative tradition. Consequently, I have been freer than Finger to point to the internal problems with the various traditional motifs, and also to emphasize that their historical relationship (ransom theory rejected by Anselm who is rejected by Abelard) makes it impossible to synthesize these motifs without doing violence to their own claims for themselves. Finger's new construction always reflects earlier elements so that the new also looks a lot like the past. In contrast, I have been much freer than Finger to attempt a new construction of atonement not beholden to the received tradition of doctrine, but that clearly reflects Jesus' rejection of violence. I have also been much freer to abandon some atonement motifs as no longer serviceable rather than treating the history of atonement doctrines as a source from which I should incorporate as many elements, if redefined, as possible.

These differences of methodology have far greater implications than can be explored in this brief response. These differences aside, however, I fully agree with Finger's conclusion that *Christus Victor* is the atonement motif best able to reflect the nonviolence that is intrinsic to the narrative of Jesus.

Response to Thomas Finger
Hans Boersma

There is a great deal in Thomas Finger's chapter that I warmly endorse. His authentically Irenaean *Christus Victor* model imports several healthy correctives to one-sidedly substitutionary and moral influence theories. I am thinking, for instance, of Finger's view of disobedience as greed, casting human beings in the role not only of willful rebels, but also of victims in bondage. I have in mind also the transformative dimension of the *Christus Victor* theme, leading to human deification.[1] And, finally, I think of Finger's emphasis on Christ's resurrection as his victory over death. Finger's appropriation of Irenaeus's recapitulation theory does not take the form of a radical reworking in which the powers of evil are demythologized into oppressive structures and institutions and in which Jesus' conflict with evil powers is reduced to a moral example. Instead, Finger presents us with a robust presentation of the ancient recapitulation theory, which opens up a great deal of opportunity for fruitful discussion.

Finger identifies this Irenaean recapitulation theory mainly with the *Christus Victor* theme. To be sure, he acknowledges the mimetic value of moral influence theories and agrees that the notion of "substitution" has its place (as long as it is not understood as an extrinsic transfer that does not transform human beings). He even allows for the notions of divine judgement and punishment. Nonetheless, I wish Finger would be more explicit about connecting Irenaeus's recapitulation theory not only with the *Christus Victor* theme, but also with the moral influence and satisfaction theories. With regard to the latter, while acknowledging in a footnote that God at times does punish directly (e.g., his punishment of Uzzah in 2 Sam. 6), Finger maintains that "God normally judges sin *indirectly*: by handing people over to the lords they choose."[2] As a result, Finger is rather circumspect in the way he describes the Father's involvement in the cross. Speaking of the powers of evil, Finger comments that "Jesus bore *their* wrath, *not* his Father's, *directly*."[3] Finger does acknowledge—and I am grateful for the recognition—that the Father used the powers to execute his justice, and that God was involved to the extent that he is involved in everything: God continued to govern the universe, also with respect to the crucifixion of Jesus. In other words, Finger acknowledges a general or universal providential guidance, which includes the Father leading the Son on his journey to the cross, and that includes the judgment of the Father's deliberate abandonment of Jesus at the cross. We could perhaps describe this in the Augustinian sense as a *permissio activa*, so that it is the evil powers who execute Jesus, but who do so under the overall control and government of God.

Finger's acceptance of the notion of divine punishment—at times direct punishment—and of divine intentionality in the cross is significant because it implies a modification of his otherwise uncompromising nonviolent stance. But I would urge him to be more liberal with the notion of divine punishment (and, hence, divine violence). As it is, he states that "God, on one level, allows other powers to punish sin, ultimately with eternal death. Yet on a deeper level God works to save those under their judgment."[4] This two-tiered description of what happens in situations like judgment (including the crucifixion) is an attempt to keep the responsibility for Jesus' death restricted to the evil powers while at the same insisting that God uses their agency to effect salvation. But this separation between two tiers (God and evil powers) is not as neat a distinction as Finger would have us believe. In the statement I just quoted, Finger insists that the evil *powers* are the ones punishing. Elsewhere, however, he is forced to admit that God does not only use the evil powers' agency for his own salvific purposes, but that his active permission is such that he himself can be said to punish (indirectly, and so by means of evil powers). In other words, at times Finger admits that God's involvement is not restricted to him simply *using* the (otherwise independent) evil acts of other powers, but that he actually himself hands people over to these evil powers. God's permission thus turns out to be a very *active* permission, which hardly avoids intentionality and hence responsibility. The two tiers end up so closely intertwined that I cannot see why Finger would still object to the language of "divine punishment" on the cross.

Unfortunately, Finger's reticence in using this language makes it difficult for him to positively speak of divine intentionality in the cross. The issue comes down to God's role in judgment and punishment. To my mind, divine wrath does not express itself merely by allowing human actions to reap their harvest of natural consequences. Divine wrath involves more than God passively "handing over" sinners to the natural consequences of their actions. In a superb essay on the relationship between God's love and wrath, Tony Lane points out that throughout the New Testament, God quite actively shows his anger (Acts 5:1-11; 12:23; Rom. 1:24, 26, 28; 3:5; 12:19; 1 Cor. 10:22; 11:30; 2 Thess. 1:7-9; Rev. 2:22-23).[5] Presenting a devastating critique of C. H. Dodd's view of divine anger as an impersonal process of cause and effect, Lane comments sharply that we are far too inclined to look for "a God whose purpose is to serve humanity," whose function is "to stand surety for human purposes," and who in his tolerance "respects human rights."[6] Lane argues instead that love without wrath is impossible and that failure to hate evil "implies a deficiency in love."[7] So, if we are to retain the primacy of God's love as his essential characteristic, we dare not avoid the corollary that this love implies anger against sin. To be sure, Finger accepts that the cross is the outcome of God's judgement against sin. And I suspect that he may well regard divine wrath as a personal affection rather than a merely impersonal effect. But one cannot help wonder about the reality of such personal affection if it is true that God generally refuses to act on it by punishing in a direct fashion. Does not the love of parental discipline involve the willingness to punish? Likewise, we need to uphold divine punishment as the outcome of his wrath in order to safeguard the love of God.

Notes

1. I am not sure what Finger means with Jesus' divinization as "the first human to be entirely at-oned with God" and with Jesus being "increasingly divinized by God's Spirit." I wonder how he squares this with Chalcedonian Christology.

2. Finger, 94. Daniels works with a similar understanding of divine wrath as God giving the creation up to its own desires (Rom. 1).

3. Ibid., 98.

4. Ibid., 94.

5. Tony Lane, "The Wrath of God as an Aspect of the Love of God," in *Nothing Greater, Nothing Better: Theological Essays on the Love of God*, ed. Kevin J. Vanhoozer (Grand Rapids: Eerdmans, 2001), 151-52.

6. Ibid., 153-54.

7. Ibid., 160.

Response to Thomas Finger
T. Scott Daniels

In the first season of *Joan of Arcadia*, God (in one of his many forms) came to Joan and asked her—without further explanation—to find a way to remove a sculpture, crafted by her good friend Adam, from the school art show. At this point in her journey she had learned not only to listen but to obey the voice of God. However, after several failed attempts at removing the sculpture peacefully from the show, Joan finally in frustration took an iron bar and smashed the art completely. She obeyed God, but in the process, with weapon in hand, destroyed a beautiful and meaningful work of art and shattered her friendship with Adam.

God comes to Joan in her grief at the end of the episode and tells her where she failed. "Like most of the creation," he tells her, "you suffer from a horrible *failure of imagination*. Whenever you think you are out of options you immediately turn to destruction."

"Destruction," he reminds her, "is *never* an option."

If Thomas Finger's essay on *Christus Victor* were a revival sermon I would have come forward during the first verse of the invitation hymn. Finger has clearly and beautifully articulated the atonement in terms that not only make sense of the crucifixion narratives, but that encompass the depth, breadth, and mystery of the entire biblical witness concerning the nature and character of God. The life, death, and resurrection of Jesus Christ brings victory over all of the principalities and powers that hold human life captive and wage war against the kingdom of God.

I concur with nearly everything that Finger wrote concerning *Christus Victor*, but let me point out three things I found especially helpful.

1. I appreciated greatly Finger's description of atonement as "at-one-ment" and his assessment of the various theories of atonement using the criteria of their ability to articulate this "making one" of God and creation. The descriptions of the three theories of atonement and their historical backgrounds were very helpful.

2. In raising the question of how things become "at-one" I believe Finger is right on the mark when he says, "*At the Gospels' heart*, then, we

find a conflict over the basic means of bringing atonement: by war and domination, or by servanthood and the way of peace."[1] I can't help thinking of the dramatic contrast in the Garden of Gethsemane between the cup of suffering Jesus drinks and the sword of Peter.

3. Finger's description of justice as "handing sinners over to the lords they choose" is a much more consistent understanding of God's justice than is found in most substitutionary theories. This view also seems to be biblically consistent with God's permitting Israel to receive the consequences of choosing kingship in the Old Testament (1 Sam. 8) and Paul's description of divine judgment upon the wicked in Romans 1 as God's "giving them up" to the powers of their choosing.

Beyond these aspects of the essay that I found especially helpful, this essay also leads me to three areas for further thought and dialogue.

1. Those like myself in the Wesleyan tradition should find this kind of understanding of the atonement very persuasive and helpful. Several recent Wesley scholars, such as Randy Maddox, have argued that the Wesleyan understanding of sanctification has much of its grounding in the Eastern tradition of Christianity—particularly the idea of divinization.[2] In my opinion, the Wesleyan doctrine of sanctification has struggled for credibility in part because it does not work within the juridical models of the West. But sanctification as the process of divinization or complete realization of divine lordship—in terms such as those articulated here by Finger—open great possibilities for a renewed understanding of holiness that is social and relational in nature.

2. Finger points out that the *Christus Victor* model brings together the life, death, and resurrection of Christ into a cohesive unit. I believe that it also helps us read the Old Testament (as he demonstrated in his readings of Genesis) in ways that have often been overlooked. A theory of atonement that takes the powers seriously is able to see the function of the Canaanites, the Egyptians, the Babylonians, and other "powers" confronting Israel as the primary sources of conflict and temptation for the people of God as they attempt to reflect his character in an increasingly oppressive world. It also gives us the lens to read Revelation as the language of unmasking the powers or beasts that seek to possess or mark the life of the believer.

3. I wonder if the increased suspicion of theories of substitution and the attraction to theories of nonviolence and relational healing has to do in part with the increasing marginalization of Christianity to the political edges. Perhaps our loss of cultural and political influence is allowing us to hear the gospel again from the margins. It is difficult to conceive of a God who moves among the powerless and identifies with history's victims when the church is in a position of Constantinian power. Perhaps the blessing of being resident aliens is it allows us to find God again among the exiles, the oppressed, the poor, and the needy.

With Finger I agree that we have too long separated nonviolence from the center of the atonement. The church has suffered from a continual "failure of imagination" as we have confronted the principalities and powers. But perhaps a fresh nonviolent understanding of what it means to call Jesus Christ "Lord" will give us the ability to participate in the ushering in of the kingdom of God.

Notes

1. Finger, 97.
2. See Randy L. Maddox, *Responsible Grace: John Wesley's Practical Theology* (Nashville: Kingswood Books, 1994).

CHAPTER 4

PASSING THE PEACE: WORSHIP THAT SHAPES NONSUBSTITUTIONARY CONVICTIONS

T. Scott Daniels

Worship has been a point of contention for Christians of every variety for the last couple of decades. Churches in every denomination have become painfully divided over worship that their parishioners complain is too liturgical, too contemporary, too loud, too soft, too repetitive, too performance-oriented, too unprofessional, and a whole list of other "toos" too numerous to mention. But have you ever heard anyone complain that Christian worship has become too substitutionary?

That is essentially the complaint I would like to lodge here.

Is worship—as one of the defining practices of Christian community[1]— an expression of the deepest beliefs of God's people, or is worship a practice that shapes and informs the basic convictions of the Christian community? The answer is yes on both counts. Worship is a communal expression of what we believe to be most true, but the practice of worship also molds the worldview and convictions of the Body of Christ. Worship is "the church's faith in motion."[2]

An earlier draft of this essay was coauthored with Marty Michelson. I thank him for his assistance.

For this reason I would not only like to critique forms of worship I believe to be "too substitutionary" and critique the theology that informs those practices, I also would like to advocate practices of worship that form a different view of the atonement in the church and argue that the oldest and most sacramental practices of worship—namely Eucharist and Baptism—are designed to form nonsubstitutionary convictions in us.

My discussion of worship and atonement will begin with a description of what I see as the fundamental problem in contemporary worship and evangelism, namely that rather than calling believers to participate in the reconciling work of God in the world, much of contemporary worship practices distance us from that work and make us at best appreciative observers of Christ's redemption. In the second section of this essay I will describe the work of René Girard as a potential alternative for understanding the work of God in Christ in atonement; and in the final portion I will describe how sacramental forms of worship are essentially nonsubstitutionary in their form and how they are both the hope and pattern for a worship that shapes proper convictions in the Body of Christ.

Worship and the Disciple's Cross

If any want to become my followers, let them deny themselves and take up their cross daily and follow me.—Luke 9:23

The call by Jesus for his disciples to take up their cross and follow him is repeated in each of the synoptic Gospels.[3] Taking up the cross of Christ was understood as a call to participate in the reconciling mission and work of God in Christ in the world. As John Howard Yoder has described it:

> The cross of Christ was not an inexplicable or chance event, which happened to strike him, like illness or accident. To accept the cross as his destiny, to move toward it and even to provoke it, when he could well have done otherwise, was Jesus' constantly reiterated free choice; and he warns his disciples lest their embarking on the same path be less conscious of its costs (Luke 14:25-33). The cross of Calvary was not a difficult family situation, not a frustration of visions of personal fulfillment, a crushing debt or a nagging in-law; it was the political, legally to be expected result of a moral clash with the powers ruling his society.[4]

Understanding the significance of the cross—and the call for the disciple to bear one's cross—in this manner is highly problematic for substitutionary theories of atonement.

What I am describing as "substitutionary" theological frameworks are those traditional theological systems that have attempted to understand God's activity in atonement in terms of sacrificial substitution or penal satisfaction. In these traditional interpretations, Christ becomes either the one who is "punished" by God for the sin of humankind or the one who pays a debt or ransom, thus nullifying the judgment of death placed upon humanity by God. Thus in these substitutionary theories of atonement the cross becomes the location for the satisfaction of either the justice of God or the setting for a subversive transaction between the power of good against the power of evil.

If this is the case, then the call for disciples to take up their cross, in the same manner in which Jesus has taken up his, is extremely convoluted. If the role of the cross in atonement was to appease the wrath of God, then taking up our cross as disciples would imply that we are to daily take up the instrument through which God's wrath is nullified. That would make little or no sense because substitutionary atonement is dependent first upon the purity of Christ as a worthy sacrifice or substitution for the sins of humankind, and second the theory implies that the death of Christ has finally appeased God's wrath and thus no further satisfaction is necessary. Thus if the cross is understood simply as an instrument of the pouring out of God's violence upon the second person of the Trinity, then it would make no sense at all for disciples to take up their cross in a like manner. Either the disciple's cross must be understood as something different than the cross of Jesus, or there must be something incomplete—or wrong—with interpreting the cross of Jesus as an instrument for the appeasing of God's anger and justice.

Because this has been the dominant view theologically for many if not most Christian traditions, this interpretation of the atonement has also shaped the framework and imaginative lens for the practices of worship and evangelism. This seems particularly true in current evangelical worship trends that center primarily on praise to God for the payment or cancellation of a debt owed. The posture of worship seems to also translate into forms of Christian evangelism that equate a saving faith with cognitive assent or personal trust in Christ's atoning sacrifice.

We can demonstrate our point by looking at the theology of an extremely popular recent worship chorus. The words of the chorus are:

> Lord, I lift Your name on high;
> Lord, I love to sing Your praises;
> I'm so glad You're in my life;
> I'm so glad *You* came to save us.
> *You* came from Heaven to earth to show the way,
> From the earth to the cross, my debt to pay.
> From the cross to the grave, from the grave to the sky;
> Lord, I lift *Your* name on high![5]

In this chorus the theological understanding of the atonement is straightforwardly substitutionary—Christ came from heaven to the cross in order to pay a debt we could not pay on our own. Beyond the theological orientation and education that is, in my opinion, suspect, what concerns me more is the kind of community this worship posture forms. To borrow from the work of Alasdair MacIntyre—who is deeply dependent upon the work of Ludwig Wittgenstein—repeated intentional "practices" constitute the identity of a particular community. At a basic level a community shares a common language and common practices. This is what ethicists refer to as a "form of life."[6]

The form of life that is created in this kind of worship is one of distance. The emphasis in this chorus is solely on the work of Christ. Notice that each phrase celebrates how glad we are that "you" (Christ) came, "you" saved, and thus we lift "your" name on high. I do not want to be misunderstood. There is an appropriate place for praise of this nature. It is right and good for the community of Christ to celebrate all that Christ has done. But it is my sense that this posture of praise has become the dominant mode of worship in many if not most modern churches, and thus the "form of life" that the community embodies is one that stands at a distance, thanking God for what was accomplished in Christ, but fails to ever participate in that work. In other words, it is one thing to thank and praise Christ for taking up his cross, it is another thing altogether for the disciple to take up his or her cross and follow him.

Again it is not my desire to see practices of communal praise done away with. That would create—in Wittgenstein's terms—a "form of life" that would itself be antithetical to the posture of gratitude that the gospel demands. My concern is that the dominance of praise as the primary practice of worship has not only been informed by a substitutionary theology—and thus continues to form our convictions in that theological framework—but that this kind of worship shaped by a substitutionary theology creates a form of life within the Christian community that moves it away from radical redemptive participation in the world—a continuing of the ministry of the cross—into a form of life that simply gives cognitive assent at a distance to a work understood as accomplished in the death of Christ, on my behalf, in substitution for me—but essentially finished.

Various critiques by marginalized groups and an evangelically fresh reading of the Canonical texts are persuading many Christians to understand God's atoning work as victim of violence—and thus victor over violence— not as victor through violence. Using the literary and anthropological work of René Girard as a starting point, I would like to argue not only for a nonsubstitutionary theory of atonement, but I would also like to suggest practices of worship that might be constituted from such a view.

René Girard

Raymund Schwager, Marlin Miller, Robin Collins, and Anthony Bartlett have each published work on issues of atonement that use or employ René Girard and a Girardian hypothesis as a basis for talking about atonement categories.[7] My suggestion to use a Girardian hypothesis for atonement will be informed by their categories. It should be stated at the outset, as well, that there is no "Girardian theory" per se of the atonement articulated by Girard himself. However, Robin Collins has identified two "theories of atonement" that are found between Girard and his followers. He articulates these as the imitation theory and the unmasking theory.[8]

Imitation

Mimesis—Girard's preferred term for the imitative kinds of acts or desires that happen between persons—is the primary category for understanding the patterns of violence that have plagued all of human history. Prior to Girard, the social sciences tended to blame the high degree of violence among human beings as the result of aggression. The problem Girard sees with the assumption about aggression is that it is too one-sided: "It aggressively divides mankind between the aggressors and the aggressed, and we include ourselves in the second category. But most human conflicts are two-sided, reciprocal."[9] In essence, Girard argues that humans are competitive rivals who mimetically imitate one another because we seek the same object, goal, or agenda. We do not know what to desire, so to find out we watch the people we admire and imitate their desires.

The imitation of one another escalates as the mimetic rivalry between the competitors grows. The rivalrous relationship continues and there is a sense of merging—a oneness of opinion or desire by the rivals. "The imitator becomes the model of his model, and model the imitator of his imitator."[10] The reality that both persons want the same goal, object, or agenda creates a loss of distinction between the persons. Whereas they are clearly not the "same" person, their plans and perspectives are the same. This imitative rivalry, compounded by a sense of lost self to the other's goals, creates an irresolvable conflict that inevitably leads to murderous violence. One or the other rival must be removed.

Girard believes that these mimetic rivalries can become so intense and contagious that they not only lead to murder between rivals, but they more often than not spread to entire communities. Brother becomes mimetic rival of brother. Nation becomes mimetic rival of nation.

Given the escalation of mimetic rivalry, the species could have or maybe should have come to utter annihilation. But it hasn't. Why not? Girard hypothesizes (based on the work of various cultural myths) that it is at the point of irresolvable conflict that an alternative emerges. The alternative does not "free" the tension of rivalry and conflict—it redirects it. The redirection of this violence is against a separate victim, the scapegoat.

According to Girard the birth of the most ancient religious myths came out of a need to redirect mimetic rivalry in order to save the human species from its violence. The most ancient of these religious myths tend to justify forms of communal and mob violence by portraying a guilty victim or bona fide troublemaker. These myths paint the victims of violence

130

as foreigners, as monsters, or as stereotyped participants in rape, infanticide, bestiality, and so forth.[11] These mythical victims also often bear physical impairments. They have one eye, a hunched back, or are crippled.

For Girard, these justifying claims were not true; indeed, it is important to Girard's theory that they are false. As he states, "It was not the discovery of some authentic criminal, as claimed by myths, that reconciled these archaic communities; it was the illusion of such a discovery. The communities mimetically transferred all their hostilities to the single victim and became reconciled on the basis of the resulting illusion."[12] The result of the act of violence against this guilty victim is found in the Greek word *catharsis*. The rivalrous tension of the community is cleansed in a single act of violence. "The unanimous mimetic contagion transforms the disastrous violence of *all against all* into the healing violence of *all against one*. The community is reconciled at the cost of one victim only."[13]

The Scapegoat

The next evolutionary step in the development of religion for Girard occurs when the now reconciled communities come to understand their newfound peace—at the cost of the victim—as a form of the miraculous. This miraculous reconciliation becomes a moment of remembrance and ritual.

The Old Testament narrative of Jonah can be seen as one of many examples of scapegoating for Girard.[14] Faced with a potentially destructive storm, understood by the sailors as a form of divine retribution, the crew is faced with the destruction of its community: "The ship represents the community, the tempest the sacrificial crisis."[15] The sailors cast lots, and the lot fell upon Jonah.[16] The crew heading to Tarshish tries to make it to the shore, attempting to save Jonah's life. But they finally recognize the futility of their efforts, address God to explain their innocence in the process, and proceed to cast Jonah into the sea, followed by further sacrifices unto the Lord.[17]

As Girard describes, "What we see here is a reflection of the sacrificial crisis and its resolution. The victim is chosen by lot; his expulsion saves the community, as represented by the ship's crew; and a new god is acknowledged through the crew's sacrifice to the Lord whom they did not know before."[18] This "sacrificial crisis" is repeated and relived, according to Girard, in the history of cultures as complex as Greek culture[19] and as primitive as the Chukchi culture.[20] The sacrificial crisis within a culture can take on the formal rituals of the human sacrifice ceremonies of the Aztecs or can be as subtle as the persecution of the Jews during the Black Death plagues in the north of France during the fourteenth century.[21] As the classic literature of China recognizes regarding the propitiatory function of sacrificial rites, "Such practices 'pacify the country and make the people settled.... It is through the sacrifices that the unity of the people is strengthened.'"[22]

Girard believes the development of ritual sacrifice to be the most important religious institution in human history. From this point in religious history on, ancient cultures ritually sacrifice victims—or scapegoats—in the hope of preventing mimetic conflicts. Violence is enacted against an outside entity, but not arbitrarily. Girard demonstrates that the violence perpetrated upon the victim or scapegoat brings a resolution to the rivalry through enacted violence.[23] Further, the "achievement" of the scapegoat is not only the appeasing of the rivalrous conflict but the unmasking of the victimizer(s), thus causing the victim to be perceived anew. Whereas the scapegoat is still victim, the scapegoat becomes in one and the same act the "god" who rescues the rivals from their violent crisis.

Thus in Girardian terms what Jesus does in allowing himself to be scapegoated by the crowd is to participate in the scapegoat mechanism as victim. He sides with the victim at the hands of the violent victimizers. In so doing, Jesus' willing death at the hands of the angry mob becomes God's identification with the suffering death that brings healing to the violence inherent in all cultures. Jesus' death does not, surely, stop the scapegoat mechanism from happening after his own death—we need only look to Acts chapters 7 and 8 to see it operative in the martyrdom of Stephen. But, by his willing participation in the scapegoat mechanism, Jesus frees humanity from the need to continually participate in patterns of rivalrous mimesis that lead to death. In so doing, Jesus detoxifies the violence and sets the model by which mimetic rivalry can and should be cured.

132

Jesus' life and teaching, in the view of Girard, is not seen as a judgment from God on the systems of the world per se. Rather, Girard sees the apocalyptic judgment passages of Jesus[24] as Jesus' proclamation of a realistic appraisal of the functions and purposes of life in the systems and structures of the day. Thus, the "judgment" in these passages is not so much God's direct and wrathful condemnation but is the result of human actions that fall down upon themselves.[25] In the language of Romans chapter 1, God's "wrathful" judgment is giving the creation up to its own desires. Hence, the cross is not needed to prevent or stop God's judgment—permitting the principalities and powers of the world to violently turn in upon themselves. The cross of Christ is necessary for exposing mimetic violence, thus ending the judgment inherent in the very violent structures of life itself.

Again, for Girard, Jesus did not have to die in order to stop God's judgment, but instead Jesus "has to die because continuing to live would mean a compromise with violence. . . . Here we have the difference between the religions that remain subordinated to the powers and the act of destroying those powers through a form of transcendence that never acts by means of violence, is never responsible for any violence, and remains radically opposed to violence."[26]

In the logic of Girard, the victimization of Jesus is not mere accident or charade. In his life Jesus clearly identified with the marginalized, the outsider, and the victim.[27] As Schwager argues, Jesus was not just a random victim or a passive one, but a participatory victim insofar as Jesus exposed the will of the people to kill.[28] Schwager goes on to argue that in killing Jesus, the participants (and in the Gospels all participate) declare judgment on themselves by forcing (or attempting to force) God's hand and God's will. "By identifying with sinners and accepting their judgment, Jesus transforms that judgment into something else: he opens a new way of salvation, a way dependent not on compromise with violence and deceit but on the resurrection and the sending of the Holy Spirit."[29]

Therefore, God's response to the violence is not to stop it and the mechanism associated with it, but to become the victim of it, and to redeem it by raising Jesus from the dead. The cross and death of Jesus expose what every generation—as a mimetic culture—would do to Jesus: crucify him. But in the proclamation of the Christ event we see the injustice of the systems in which we participate—systems of acquisition, power, and prominence—wherein we, like the crowd, crucify the victims in our midst. In seeing that scapegoat mechanism revealed, we recognize the categories of atonement offered. That is, we see the ways in which we would be and are participants in this mimetic rivalrous process and we receive the disciple's call to take up our cross and participate in the scapegoat's transcendence of this process through nonviolence.

Assessing Girard

A theory—like Girard's—that attempts to be universal and comprehensive in its scope is always open for critique. Although I agree with the critiques of Girard offered by scholars such as Walter Wink[30] and Paul Keim,[31] I also agree that Girard may help us interpret human violence and the depth of the gospel in ways that have largely been overlooked.

What we find most helpful in Girard is an articulation of the Christian gospel that "understands the Hebrew Bible as a long and laborious exodus out of the world of violence and sacred projections, an exodus plagued by many reversals and falling short of its goal."[32] Girard's scapegoat theory lends to us a language and lens that understands the violent human process of desire that breaks relationship between Adam and Eve, incites the murderous violence of Cain against Abel, leads Lamech to sing his hypnotic song of massive retribution to his children, corrupts and fills the entire culture of Noah with violence, and forms artificial boundaries and barriers between cultures after Babel.

As Raymund Schwager and others have pointed out, in Girard we find a way of interpreting the often embarrassing violence of the Old Testament as "the residue of false ideas about God carried over from the general human past."[33] It is important, however, to recognize the seeds in the Old Testament of the unmasking of the scapegoating system. For example, the most violent accounts within the Hebrew Scriptures—with only a few exceptions—occur in the context of a violence that is administrated by human hands, and is seen as self-destructive. A great example of unmasked, self-destructive violence is Gideon's war against the Midianites in Judges 7. While Gideon's army of "dogs" surrounded the Midian camp and waged war by holding torches, smashing jugs, and blowing trumpets, the violence of the enemy turned in upon itself.[34]

What is unique in Girard is the understanding that the gospel from Judaism to Jesus is not just one more myth among many, but it is a "counterforce in our universe that tends toward the revelation of the immemorial lie."[35] Walter Wink summarizes Girard's perspective on the violence of the Scripture best:

> The violence of the Bible is the necessary precondition for the gradual perception of its meaning. The scapegoat mechanism could have come to consciousness only in a violent society. The problem of violence could only emerge at the very heart of violence, in the most war-ravaged corridor on the globe, by a repeatedly subjugated people unable to seize and wield power for any length of time. The violence of Scripture, so embarrassing to us today, became the means by which sacred violence was revealed for what it is: a lie perpetrated against victims in the name of a God who, through violence, was working to expose violence for what it is and to reveal the divine nature as nonviolent.[36]

Girard recognizes that gradually—but finally—the entire Scripture is written from the viewpoint of the victims. Scripture sides with the persecuted. "God is revealed, not as demanding sacrifice, but as taking the part of the sacrificed. From Genesis to Revelation, the victims cry for justice and deliverance from the world of myth where they are made scapegoats. In the cross these cries find vindication."[37] For Girard, the uniqueness of the revelation of Christ is not that he is scapegoated—that process is as old as religion. What is unique is that the gospel condemns and "denounces the verdict passed by these Powers as a total miscarriage of justice, a perfect example of untruth, a crime against God."[38]

In the cross the violence of humanity is revealed. In the cross that violence is met by a God who is revealed in a grace that refrains from retribution and needs no act of violence in return to make restitution. In God's act of identification with the scapegoats of history, he has exposed the system as a lie and has revealed a different pattern of living that can only be described as "the way, the truth, and the life."

Those who call Christ "Lord" must take up their cross—their willingness to witness that the systems of dominance and violence are false—and follow him. Pentecost as well is then understood as the empowering of the Body of Christ to reverse the effects of Babel by embodying a people free of the false borders created through mimetic rivalry of nation against nation.

Some may criticize a theory based on Girardian language and theory as simply a restatement of Abelard's "moral influence" theory. If this is the case, then the death of Christ was nothing more than a moral pattern for life. Although I recognize the call to carry the disciple's cross must include the crucifixion as some form of moral influence, with scholars like Wink I would argue that Girard's theory opens new possibilities for understanding Christ as *Christus Victor*. Substitutionary forms of atonement have often acted in highly individualistic ways—offering a transaction of reconciliation between God and the believer. For Girard, what Christ does is expose the "powers" to which we are held captive. It is true that we have rebelled against God, but that is not the sole source of our alienation. "It is also the result of our being socialized by alienating rules and requirements. We do not freely surrender our authenticity; it is stolen from us by the Powers."[39]

So why is the death of Christ necessary? Because the cross unmasks and defeats "the Powers" that hold us captive and separate us from God. As Schwager puts it, "God needs no reparation, but human beings must be extracted from their own prison if they are to be capable of accepting the pure gift of freely offered love. . . . It is not God who must be appeased, but humans who must be delivered from their hatred."[40]

What becomes critical to worship in this understanding of the atonement Jesus offers is the manner in which the atonement offered calls for a recapitulating and participating response in working out the effects of atonement. That is, we dare not say that we "work" out our own salvation or we "bring" our own salvation. But, there is a means by which we are called to be participants in the life and death of Christ in order to further actualize the atoning work of God in the world. The atoning work of Christ frees humankind from the mimetic crisis and in so doing calls the disciples of Christ to a mimesis of his life. To take up one's own cross is thus a call to a participatory cross-purposed life—a life that lives intentionally against the violent patterns and systems of life such that we affect a kind of atonement in our lifestyle.

In the same way that the Hebraic tradition understands the creating process of God as incomplete apart from the cocreating work of humankind to multiply and fill the earth, a nonsubstitutionary articulation of the atonement understands the atonement as having taken place but remaining incomplete apart from the participation in God's atoning work by the disciple. Like the kingdom of God that is both already present, but not yet fully revealed, our life—imitative of his life—completes redemption in a world that clearly continues to participate in violent overthrow, acquisitive consumerism, and rivalrous fratricide. And so it is to the importance of worship—what we have described as "passing the peace"—that we return now.

Passing the Peace

It ought to be clear to the reader at this point that I not only believe that a nonviolent theory of the atonement is the best way to interpret the death of Christ upon the cross, but that it also serves as the model for disciples of the nonviolent participation in the world that the gospel requires. A nonviolent understanding of the cross cannot simply stand in awe of the nonretributive grace of the crucifixion and resurrection, but it logically includes the call for those who are part of the Body of Christ to extend that same grace into the world today. So given this nonsubstitutionary perspective on the atonement, how ought the practices of worship and evangelism be different? How can our practices of worship form us into people who know how to pass the peace?

It should come as no surprise that we might suggest beginning with the sacraments. Christians broadly agree that the primary sacraments of baptism and Eucharist constitute the church. One becomes a member of the church by being baptized, and the Eucharist defines the fellowship of the church.[41] Both are means of grace through which we participate in the atoning work of God in the world.

Beyond reaffirming a nonsubstitutionary view or being an addition to a non-violent view of the atonement, it could be argued that the sacraments are our best argument for a nonsubstitutionary understanding of the death of Christ. It would not be the first time that the sacraments were used as an argument for a particular theological view.[42] In the fourth-century debates over the doctrine of the Trinity, Athanasius argued for the divinity of the Holy Spirit based upon the fact that for at least a couple of centuries the church had baptized believers in the names of the Father, Son, and Holy Spirit. "The baptismal formula itself constituted a proof. Without the name of the Holy Spirit the formula would be incomplete and therefore the baptism invalid."[43]

It is not from the formulas of Eucharist and baptism that we would like to argue that they articulate a nonviolent theory of atonement, but it is from the posture and call to participation of both sacraments that a participatory nonviolent understanding of atonement grows. We do not come to acts of liturgy primarily to be changed as individuals. We come to encounter God. However, when God is encountered rightly, a new reality emerges, a new people is formed. As Robert Webber and Rodney Clapp have argued, "The transformation of the church is a by-product of the liturgy. It occurs only when the church is determined foremost simply to worship God."[44]

Baptism

Baptism is not an act of observation. "Baptism is participation—intelligent, full-bodied, wholehearted participation."[45] In baptism the believer enacts the entire story of the gospel by identifying his or her life with the life of Christ. In the words of Paul, "Do you not know that all of us who have been baptized into Christ Jesus were baptized into his death? Therefore we have been buried with him by baptism into death, so that, just as Christ was raised from the dead by the glory of the Father, so we too might walk in newness of life" (Rom. 6:3-4).

The meaning of baptism has its roots in concepts of primeval chaos. It is against the waters of chaos—the *tohu vabohu* of Genesis 1:2—that God speaks order into existence. Out of the waters of chaos creation is formed. In the narratives of Noah we find that the breath of God again sweeps over the waters of chaos—the consequence of a creation "filled with violence"[46]—and brings a new creation out of the flood waters of destruction.[47]

Later when Israel faced the waters of chaos on one side and the chaos of the violent enemy on the other, the breath of God again swept across the face of the waters and formed a new creation—a people redeemed from the powerful systems of violence and slavery—set free to be a people shaped by covenant with God.

John's baptism became a way for people to identify with this redemptive history of Israel. The baptism of John was associated with repentance and turning from the systems of sin and violence in order to identify and participate with God's redeemed people in the world. It is along these same lines that Paul and the New Testament church "can speak of conversion and baptism creating a new person—even a new world (2 Cor. 5:17). The biological family, let alone the nation-state, is no longer the primary source of identity, support and growth."[48]

I believe that this understanding of baptism as a primary practice of identification and participation in the death and resurrection of Jesus Christ is highly instructive for a theology of atonement. In Girardian terms, in baptism we have participated in the death of the scapegoat through mutual identification with Christ-as-victim, and in that practice have not only exposed but put to death the previous mimetic patterns of our sinful existence whose ultimate wages are death. In other words, in baptism the world of chaos and violence that has been exposed in the crucifixion of Christ—the world of *tohu vabohu*; of creation-corrupting violence; of principalities and powers like Egypt; of violent oppressive Rome; and of confining religious fundamentalism—has been put to death in the life of the believer, and the resurrection life of Christ and the community of his kingdom has been brought to life.

Baptism does not allow believers to stand at a distance and simply praise God the Father for the substitutionary sacrifice of God the Son; it requires that we identify ourselves with that same death in order that we might share in his new life.

Eucharist

Although it certainly takes a lifetime—or more—to learn to live into the one-time act of baptism, the Eucharist, however, is a constant and continual sacrament that the Christian community submits themselves to again and again. In Eucharist, we participate in a vivid practice that reminds us of our culpability in the death of Christ, and also of the transformation of life made possible by his sacrificial grace.

Eucharist is certainly a meal of remembrance and praise. (The term *Eucharist* literally means "thanksgiving".) However, the Lord's Table invites us to a particular kind of remembering. It is a remembering that invites us to participation—to a taking in to our selves that which we remember.

In 1 Corinthians 11 Paul is very upset with the church because when they gather together for the Lord's Supper they eat the meal in such a way that they "drink judgment against themselves" (v. 29). Apparently some in the church had begun to turn the sacrament into a meal of individual grace, and thus they were partaking of the bread and the wine before the others arrived. Failure to wait, failure to include everyone, is a failure to "discern the body" (v. 29). Their problem is not that they do not take the Eucharist with enough seriousness; their problem is that they "misunderstand that the focus of communion is not upon some magical, heavenly food but rather upon Christ and their brothers and sisters around the table who have been saved, called, and gifted by Christ and formed into his 'body.' "[49]

The reason that failure to "discern the body" brings condemnation upon the church is because disunity continues the very destruction we are called to the table to remember. As we hold the symbols of broken body and shed blood, we are collectively reminded of both our proclivity and culpability in violence and destruction as well as the atoning grace of God that reconciles enemies and overcomes violence through grace.

Again to use Girardian terms, when the church gathers around the table of the Lord we are made keenly aware that our life together is not possible apart from the peacemaking scapegoating of the one whose body was broken and whose blood was shed. However, the partaking of the scapegoat's body and blood into our own bodies is a mimetic practice done in the hope that our lives will somehow, by grace, be transformed into a replication of his life. Our hope in Eucharist is that we will become what we eat; we will be made the Body of Christ.

Evangelism and Other Forms of Liturgy

Beyond the sacraments, our other forms of liturgy ought, as much as possible, call us to participate in the atoning work of Christ as well. Because the reconciling work of God is, in one sense, complete in the death of Christ, praise to God for his work in salvation is not invalid, or unimportant. My complaint that worship has become too substitutionary is not a desire to have praise eliminated from the worship of the Christian community, but it is a call to move beyond praise to recognize the need for regular and intentional acts of participation and identification in our worship and liturgy.[50]

Let me conclude with an example of a liturgy of participation. It is the regular practice of my local congregation to participate in responsive readings during the Lenten season. One of the Lenten readings based on passages from the New International Version of the Bible goes as follows:

I am the good shepherd.

The good shepherd lays down his life for the sheep.

I have not been rebellious;
I have not drawn back.

I offered my back to those who beat me.

I did not hide my face from mocking and spitting.

**He was oppressed and afflicted,
yet he did not open his mouth;**

He was led like a lamb to the slaughter,
and as a sheep before her shearers is silent,
so he did not open his mouth.

**When they hurled their insults at him,
he did not retaliate;**

When he suffered, he made no threats.
Instead, he entrusted himself to him who judges justly.

**I lay down my life—
only to take it up again.**

I am the good shepherd.

**No one takes [my life] from me,
but I lay it down of my own accord.**

Do you think I cannot call on my Father,
and he will at once put at my disposal
more than twelve legions of angels?

**But I, when I am lifted up from the earth,
will draw all men to myself.**[51]

Although this is a very beautiful reading, rich with Scripture references, there is a tendency within it, much like a song of praise, to look at the life of the one who lays down his life for others, without a call for us to participate in that same life. Rather than use that responsive reading, I wrote a different reading for the congregation. My congregation has a tradition that we walk together through all of Lent at the foot of the cross. The pulpit is removed and a large wooden cross remains in the center of the platform. Each Sunday a family processes in and lays another Lenten symbol—the nails, the bag of coins, the crown of thorns, and so forth—at the foot of the cross, and then leads the congregation in the responsive reading. The following reading was written for the third Sunday of Lent. The symbol for the day was the whip, and the text for the sermon was John 4—the Samaritan woman.

The Samaritan Woman—The Whip

Leader:
The symbol we lay before the cross today is the soldier's whip, an instrument of punishment and coercion. Today we also remember the grace Jesus freely extended to a Samaritan woman. With the whip we inflict pain on our enemy. With the whip we keep our enemy at an arm's length. In a culture that divided people because of their gender, Jesus extended grace to a woman. In a culture that viewed other races with disdain, Jesus extended love to a Samaritan.

Congregation:
Lord, Jesus Christ, when we are tempted to make the kingdom of God a place for people who look just like us, help us say no to our tendencies toward social separation.
Help us say yes to the cross.

Leader:
With the whip we try to coerce others to do our will. Jesus freely offered his love to the Samaritan woman without any threat of punishment.

Congregation:
Lord, Jesus Christ, when we are tempted to use our power to manipulate the political landscape or scare people into the kingdom of God, help us say no to the coercion of power.
Help us say yes to the cross.

Leader:
We use the whip to remind people—with pain and scars—of their trespasses. Jesus, although aware of the woman's sin, refused to condemn but only forgave.

Congregation:
Lord, Jesus Christ, when we are tempted to constantly remind our neighbor of their sin and destroy our enemy by rehearsing their past, help us say no to keeping a record of wrongs.
Help us say yes to the cross.

Leader:
The whip offers to our enemy violence and death. Jesus offered his enemy the hope of living water.

Congregation:
Lord, Jesus Christ, when we are tempted to use even our holiness to hurt the enemy, help us say no to the whip.
Help us say yes to the cross.

Leader:
Let us pray.

Congregation:
Almighty God, you know our sin. You know how we misuse our power. Our hands are full of blood. Wash us and make us clean. Help us lay down our instruments of destruction. Teach us to be a reflection

of your love and grace. Forgive us our trespasses as we forgive those who trespass against us. Mold us into the image of Jesus, in whose holy name we pray. Amen.[52]

That which applies to the liturgy worship also applies to evangelism. Worship that calls believers to participate in the ongoing redemption and atoning work of God in the world is evangelism. The church's worship is evangelism. As Stanley Hauerwas quips, "That we Methodists thought we had to erect tents to evangelize should have suggested to us that something had gone wrong with our worship."[53]

The call of Jesus for disciples to take up the cross daily and follow him should continually be a mandate that shapes our theology and our communal practices. The ability of the disciple to take up the cross must mean that there is more to the atonement than some kind of transaction of divine retribution and justice. The logic of taking up the cross must mean that the crucifixion of Christ be understood in terms like those of Girard, interpreting the death of Jesus as a radical unmasking of the principalities and powers that shape the violent structures of the world in such a way that those powers are now defeated.

I always feel a need here to speak a word of clarification about a nonviolent Christian perspective. Critics of nonviolence often raise the question of how this kind of interpretation of the gospel affects the battered wife, the abused child, or the victim of political or social injustice. Is it the will of God that persons facing various forms of violent mistreatment continue to submit themselves to repeated acts of destruction? Our obvious answer is no—they should not submit themselves to further abuse.

This is, however, a response consistent with our nonviolent view. For the power of the cross is that it exposes the lie that is the enemies' violence. The love of God in Christ not only identifies with victims, but it refuses to allow the one who misuses power to go on living unexposed. The wife who is abused by her violent husband has an obligation to that husband to not allow him to continue on in his destructive life as abuser. For the salvation of the abuser they must be exposed. Also, if Girard's theory of mimetic and sacrificial violence is right, there is an additional danger in relationships of unexposed violence that the frustrated response to the aggressor will exacerbate the violence, or that in an attempt to bring peace without truth, further violence will be deflected upon a scape-goat—for example, a child.

Perhaps this is what the apostle John meant in his prologue when he described the Word made flesh as "full of grace and truth." In the cross of Christ we at the same time see the violent and sinful truth of humankind confronted with the overwhelming and costly grace of God. In the same way, then, the life of the community of Christ walks in the light of the truth and speaks the truth in love to one another while participating in the difficult patterns and practices of forgiveness that become reflections of Christ's costly grace.

It is our hope that our practices of worship and evangelism follow the pattern of the sacraments and call believers to participate daily in the peacemaking, Spirit-empowered reconciling work of God in the world. When we come to understand what it means to be disciples in this way, we come to understand what Paul meant when he said:

> If anyone is in Christ, there is a new creation: everything old has passed away; see, everything has become new! All this is from God, who rec-onciled us to himself through Christ, and has given to us the ministry of reconciliation; that is, in Christ God was reconciling the world to himself, not counting their trespasses against them, and entrusting the message of reconciliation to us. So we are ambassadors for Christ, since God is making his appeal through us; we entreat you on behalf of Christ, be reconciled to God. (2 Cor. 5:17-20)

One of my favorite moments in chapel at the college where I worked was when one of the student worship leaders asked the congregation to close their eyes and sing together, "Open my eyes Lord, we want to see Jesus." There was for a brief humorous moment, complete communal confusion. Perhaps it makes just as much sense for us to expect the transformation of the creation while only calling disciples to stand afar off and give praise to the one who enacted atonement in the past without calling the community of Christ to participate in the ongoing nature of his redemption. We are not people who earn our salvation through practices, nor are we people who simply respond to our salvation in praise; rather we are a people engaged in salvation, working out our salvation, and calling others into this salvation through practices of kingdom allegiance.

Notes

1. I use the term *practice* here in the same way that Alasdair MacIntyre defines it, as "any coherent and complex form of socially established cooperative human activity through which goods internal to that form of activity are realized in the course of trying to achieve those standards of excellence which are appropriate to, and partially definitive of, that form of activity, with the result that human powers to achieve excellence, and human conceptions of the ends and goods involved, are systematically extended." See Alasdair MacIntyre, *After Virtue* (Notre Dame, IN: University of Notre Dame Press, 1984), 187.

2. See Aidan Kavanagh, *On Liturgical Theology* (New York: Pueblo, 1984), 73-179.

3. See Matthew 16:24; Mark 8:34; Luke 9:23 and 14:27.

4. John Howard Yoder, *The Politics of Jesus* (Grand Rapids, MI: Eerdmans, 1972), 132.

5. Rick Founds, "Lord, I Lift Your Name on High." (Emphasis mine.) See complete credit at bottom of page 128.

6. For an important description of communities and their "form of life," especially as they relate to the work of Ludwig Wittgenstein and Alasdair MacIntyre, see Fergus Kerr, *Theology After Wittgenstein* (Oxford: Basil Blackwell, 1986), or Nancey Murphy, Brad J. Kallenberg, and Mark Thiessen Nation, *Virtues and Practices in the Christian Tradition: Christian Ethics after MacIntyre* (Harrisburg: Trinity Press International, 1997), 45-81. "To share a language is to share a form of life. To share a form of life is to be a community" (p. 57).

7. Collins goes on to present his own model based on Girard's work. He calls his model the "incarnational theory." See Robin Collins, "Girard and Atonement: An Incarnational Theory of Mimetic Participation," in Willard M. Swartley, ed., *Violence Renounced: René Girard, Biblical Studies, and Peacemaking* (Telford, PA: Pandora Press, 2000), 135.

8. "Girard himself does not contend that his views provide an adequate alternative theological model for the atonement, and they in fact do not." Marlin E. Miller, "Girardian Perspectives and Christian Atonement," in Swartley, *Violence Renounced*, 46.

9. René Girard, "Violence and Religion: Cause or Effect," in *The Hedgehog Review*, vol. 6, no. 1 (Spring 2004): 9.

10. Ibid, 10.

11. For example, Girard speaks frequently of the Oedipus myth as typical of this early type of scapegoating justification.

12. Girard, "Violence and Religion," 11.

13. Ibid., 12.

14. See René Girard, *Violence and the Sacred* (Baltimore: Johns Hopkins University Press, 1972), 312-14.

15. Ibid., 313.

16. Girard believes that chance often plays an important role in the sacrificial system. A victim must be chosen in a random way that does not impose guilt upon another party. Therefore "games of chance" from casting lots to the balloon games of the Uitoto Indians become important sacrificial methods for the selection of victims. See Ibid., 311-13.

17. Jonah 1:14-16.

18. Girard, *Violence and the Sacred*, 314.

19. Girard interprets the sacrificial overtones of Greek tragedy myths such as Oedipus in great detail. See Ibid., 68-88.

20. See Ibid., 16-17, 25-28.

21. See René Girard, *The Scapegoat* (Baltimore: Johns Hopkins University Press, 1986), 1-11.

22. CH'U UY II, 2, as quoted in Girard, *Violence and the Sacred*, 8.

23. The scapegoat mechanism that Girard articulates uses the language/imagery of "the scapegoat" of Leviticus 16, but the idea of scapegoating does not emerge from this text. That is, Girard understands that the scapegoat mechanism is present in all cultures and finds its ritualized practice in cult and sacrifice.

24. See passages such as those found in Matthew 23–24, Mark 13, Luke 10, and John 8.

25. See René Girard, *Things Hidden Since the Foundation of the World* (Stanford: Stanford University Press, 1978), 203.

26. Ibid., 213-14.

27. See for example, Matthew 25:31-46, John 12:32, and so forth.

28. For example, "Woe to you! For you build the tombs of the prophets whom your ancestors killed. So you are witnesses and approve of the deeds of your ancestors; for they killed them, and you build their tombs" (Luke 11:47-48). Raymund Schwager, *Must There Be Scapegoats?* (San Francisco: Harper & Row, 1987).

29. A summary of Schwager's argument given by Marlin Miller, "Girardian Perspectives and Christian Atonement" in Swartley, *Violence Renounced*, p. 38.

30. Wink argues for the validity of Girard's theory but also gives the following points of critique. Not all myths are lies masking events of generative violence—some do tell the truth about power relations in society. Wink understands the scapegoat motif as a subset or variation on the theme of violence, and sees the combat myth of redemptive violence as more generic and common. He is not sure that the Scripture is as clear on atonement as Girard believes. Wink doubts that "the scapegoat motif is foundational for all of the world's myths, or that the Judeo-Christian Scriptures have a monopoly on the criticism of violence." He raises some historical questions for Girard regarding the history of human sacrifice; and he believes that it is risky to build an analytical theory on speculations about prehistorical culture. See Walter Wink, *Engaging the Powers: Discernment and Resistance in a World of Domination* (Minneapolis: Fortress Press, 1992), 152-55.

31. See Paul Keim, "Reading Ancient Near Eastern Literature from the Perspective of René Girard's Scapegoat Theory," in Swartley, *Violence Renounced*, 157-77.

32. Wink, *Engaging the Powers*, 146.

33. Ibid., 147.

34. Important to this narrative is the account of God's weaning of Gideon's army. Gideon began with 32,000 men and ended up with 300 who "lapped the water like dogs."

35. Girard, *The Scapegoat*, 100.

36. Wink, *Engaging the Powers*, 147.

37. Ibid.

38. Ibid., 147-48.

39. Ibid., 150.

40. Schwager, *Must There Be Scapegoats?* 209.

41. For a great discussion on the social implications of the sacraments, see Frank C.

Senn, "Sacraments and Social History: Postmodern Practice," in *Theology Today*, vol. 58, no. 3 (October 2001): 288-303.

42. It has been argued that theology always ought to begin with ethics or Christian practice rather than starting with a theological proposition and forming ethical implications. A recent scholar who has argued adamantly for ethics as the starting place of theology is James McClendon. It is the primacy of Christian ethics that caused McClendon to begin his three-volume systematic theology with a volume on ethics. See James Wm. McClendon Jr., *Systematic Theology: Ethics* (Nashville: Abingdon Press, 1986).

43. Jaroslav Pelikan, *The Christian Tradition*, Volume 1: *The Emergence of the Catholic Tradition (100-600)* (Chicago: University of Chicago Press, 1971), 217.

44. Robert E. Webber and Rodney Clapp, *People of the Truth: A Christian Challenge to Contemporary Culture* (Harrisburg, PA: Morehouse Publishing, 1988), 69.

45. Ibid., 75.

46. Genesis 6:11.

47. See Mircea Eliade, *The Sacred and the Profane* (New York: Harcourt, Brace and World, 1959), 129-36.

48. Rodney Clapp, *A Peculiar People: The Church as Culture in a Post-Christian Society* (Downers Grove, IL: InterVarsity Press, 1996), 100. Clapp goes on to argue that baptism—especially in the history of movements such as the Anabaptists—became an important form of civil disobedience. Quoting Dale W. Brown, he writes that baptism "embodied their doctrine of the church, their stance toward society, their advocacy of religious freedom, and their doctrine of separation of church and state. The baptismal rite was a powerful political act and became highly sacramental... inasmuch as it participated in the divine commissioning of disciples and Christ's baptism and suffering" (p. 101). See Dale W. Brown, "An Anabaptist Theology of the Sacraments," presidential address presented at the Midwest Section of the American Theological Society, April 25, 1986, pp. 4-5.

49. William H. Willimon, *Worship as Pastoral Care* (Nashville: Abingdon Press, 1979), 170.

50. I do not have the space here to talk in detail about preaching in ways that are "participatory" in nature. I prefer narrative forms of preaching because this style of preaching does call people ultimately to see and interpret the world through the lens of the Scripture. For an excellent example of preaching that transforms—rather than simply instructs—the church, see Charles L. Campbell, *The Word Before the Powers: An Ethic of Preaching* (Louisville: Westminster John Knox Press, 2002).

51. John 10:11; Isaiah 50:5-6; 53:7; 1 Peter 2:23; John 10:17-18; Matthew 26:53; and John 12:32.

52. Reading written by T. Scott Daniels, used at Richardson, Texas, Church of the Nazarene, copyright 2003.

53. Stanley Hauerwas, *A Better Hope: Resources for a Church Confronting Capitalism, Democracy and Postmodernity* (Grand Rapids, MI: Brazos Press, 2000), 157.

RESPONSES TO
T. SCOTT DANIELS

Response to T. Scott Daniels
J. Denny Weaver

Affirmations

I concur with T. Scott Daniels that worship is a practice that both shapes the Christian community and is an expression of the beliefs of the community. Thus I agree fully with his move to develop understandings of atonement and of worship that express the believing person's participation with and in Christ's saving work rather than focusing on a substitutionary work that Christ has accomplished in the place of the believer and that the believer appreciates from a distance. I agree that René Girard's theory of mimetic violence can make a contribution to atonement discussions, including new possibilities for understanding *Christus Victor*. As is apparent from a paragraph in my response to Hans Boersma, I agree with and use the idea that biblical pronouncements of divine judgment are "not so much God's direct and wrathful condemnation but [are] the result of human actions that fall down upon themselves."[1] I am fully in accord with Daniels that the call to "take up the cross" is a call to participate with Jesus in a life of discipleship to Jesus, "a life that lives intentionally against the violent patterns and systems of life," a life that participates in "God's atoning work" of "redemption in a world that clearly continues to participate in violent overthrow, acquisitive consumerism, and rivalrous fratricide."[2]

Points of Conversation

Although I do not dispute the overall conclusions of Daniels, I offer some different emphases and ways of getting to a similar place. I agree that Girard's theory can be a conversation partner in the discussion of atonement, but I do not believe that it is the necessary basis either for critiquing the violence of standard atonement theories or for constructing a version of *Christus Victor*. Thus I position the death and resurrection of Jesus in narrative *Christus Victor* differently than does Daniels in his version of atonement.

As I wrote in my response to Hans Boersma, a trajectory of nonviolence is visible in the Bible from creation through the eschaton. God entered human history in the call of Abraham. Abraham's calling was to become a nation in which "all the families of the earth shall be blessed" (Gen. 12:3). The narrative of those descendants of Abraham—the people of God—in the Old Testament eveals a variety of understandings of who they were in relation to God and how they should live in obedience to God. These narratives portray both violent and nonviolent initiatives, but it is Jesus' rejection of violence that reveals the trajectory through this narrative that is closest to the will of God. This track from Abraham to Jesus is a story of God's people whose mission was to witness to the reign of God in a world that did not (and still does not) recognize God's rule. God's act in Jesus was God's most complete entry into human history, but it was also a continuation and culmination that began with Abraham's call of the witness of the reign of God to and against the world that does not acknowledge the rule of God. This confrontation of reign of God and rule of evil so provoked the Powers that they—represented by Rome, the highest political authority of that era—killed Jesus. That death lasted only three days, however, for God raised Jesus from the dead, a triumph for the reign of God, and a demonstration that humankind, who shares humanity with Jesus, will one day also share in his resurrection. Thus the resurrection frees humankind from the power of death.

This interpretation places most emphasis on the life and the life-affirming witness of Jesus. One can tell this story without using Girard's theory, but I agree with Daniels that the cross reveals the violence of humanity, and that "in the cross that violence is met by a God who is revealed in a grace that refrains from retribution and needs no act of violence in return to make restitution."[3] However, I would not go so far as to say that God has identified with the scapegoats of history. Jesus' mission was to witness to the reign of God rather than to identify with the oppressed, although that mission certainly includes revealing their oppression (see Luke 4:18-19). The cross is thus not, in my view, Jesus' "willing participation in the scapegoat mechanism," but rather the event that makes clear the contrasting methodology of rule of the Powers and rule of God. One rules with violence, the other with resurrection, grace, and giving of life. Death is not part of God's plan for Jesus; Jesus' purpose was not to die so as to expose the scapegoat mechanism.

This point brings me to the difficult issue of how to answer the question of whether Jesus' death was "necessary." If Jesus' mission was the life-bringing, life-affirming mission of witnessing to the reign of God I proposed, then I cannot say that his death was intrinsically necessary to the divine will. As I wrote in my essay in this volume, understanding the action of God in Jesus within the framework of standard trinitarian theology would render it impossible to view God as a God who worked through violence. A God who intended for Jesus to die, or who set out the mission of dying to expose the scapegoat mechanism would, in my view, be a God who had a purpose in divinely intended violence. However, I am willing to say that, given the ultimate confrontation of reign of evil and reign of God that took place in the life of Jesus, his death was inevitable. The ultimate character of the confrontation made his death inevitable. To avoid death Jesus would have had to forego—fail—his mission. In order not to fail, Jesus did voluntarily choose to confront death, and one can say that God willed Jesus' death in the sense that God did not want Jesus' mission to fail. It was the circumstances of his mission rather than specific divine intent that necessitated Jesus' death. Perhaps at this point only semantics separates my formulation from that of Daniels. However, I think it important to stress that if we truly believe that the nonviolence of Jesus is an intrinsic element of the reign of God, then we need to talk about the God revealed in Jesus in ways that do not visualize God in the position of intending or needing violence to achieve purposes of the reign of God.

I agree with Daniels that in baptism we identify with the life, death, and resurrection of Jesus in order to share in his resurrected life. I push participation in the Eucharist in the same direction. We eat and drink in memory of how he faced death to carry out his mission faithfully, and we eat and drink to strengthen our own commitments to carry on that mission. That we eat and drink the body and blood of Christ reminds us that this mission is costly—carrying it on can cost us our lives—and that we consume bread and wine that nourishes our bodies and our fellowship together as the people of God who witness in the world to the reign of God.

Notes

1. Daniels, 133.
2. Ibid., 137.
3. Ibid., 135.

Response to T. Scott Daniels
Hans Boersma

Daniels contrasts worship that draws us into the redemptive narrative of the gospel through participation in the life of Christ with worship that distances and turns us into observers who praise God for an externally accomplished salvation. Whereas he regards substitutionary atonement as responsible for worship that distances, he advocates the Girardian notion of Christ's death as exposing the scapegoat mechanism, since it holds out the promise of a transformed, cross-bearing life of the Christian disciple. The contrast between distancing and participation is a thread helpfully woven throughout the chapter. Worship should indeed never be a purely intellectual or emotional response to a salvation that remains outside of us. Daniels rightly points out that worship constitutes the church's participation in the divine drama of redemption. I appreciate, therefore, the emphasis on baptism and Eucharist as practices that do not allow us to "stand at a distance" but that require us to "identify ourselves with" Christ's death, in order that we may also share in his life.

It is not so clear, however, that we should link "participation" with the unveiling of the scapegoat mechanism and that we should connect "distancing" with substitutionary atonement. Does the Girardian system escape the problem of worship from a distance? I am not convinced. According to Girard, when Christ surrenders himself to the violent death of the cross, he exposes thereby the satanic process of mutual imitation of human desires, and so conquers Satan—the personification of the process of "violent contagion."[1] So, when we ask, *How* does Christ conquer the power of evil? the answer is, by revealing or exposing that the constant imitation of human desires leads to the violence of victimizing scapegoats. It is revelation or exposing that describes the *manner* of atonement. We are to become aware of the processes of violent scapegoating and so break through the spiral of mimetic desire. The "revelation," "exposing," and "awareness" language indicates that moral influence is the deepest underlying atonement theory at work in Girard's thought.

Throughout the essay we see this moral influence theory at work. The terminology—"expose," "unmask," "revelation," "perceive," "recognize," "see," "know," and "remind"—comes straight from the Girardian moral influence textbook. But to "perceive" or "recognize" processes of imitation that lead to violence is not the same as to undo them. The problem at the heart of many moral influence theories is that they do not take seriously enough the effects of sin and evil. Girard's theory is no exception. As Hans Urs von Balthasar has pointed out, Girard has difficulty talking about sin at all, since violence is the result of a process of mimetic contagion in which *everyone* is caught up: "In [Girard's] view, the 'omnipresence of violence' means that distinction between 'good' and 'evil' is illusory. Accordingly, he does not speak of 'sin' but of 'hostility', and so forth; the concept of sin is secondary."[2] If hostility and violence resulting from imitation were indeed our only problem, moral categories might go a long way to correct things. As it is, however, the biblical notion of sin reaches deeper than violence and isn't simply the outcome of imitating one another's desires. Sin, at its heart, is the idolatrous usurpation of divinity, rendering us—to use Irenaeus's terms—corruptible and mortal. To regain eternal life much more is needed than becoming aware of our propensity to violence.

The problem with Girardian theory is that it keeps Christ at a distance. There is no participatory logic at work here, no identification between Christ and humanity. Moral influence theory, when viewed as the ultimate category of atonement theology, leads to a distancing between the Christ and those worshiping him. The praise choruses used in nonsacrificial "Girardian" churches may not sing "from the earth to the cross, my debt to pay," but they will sing, "You came from heaven to earth to show the way." It is not only celebratory praise for an external past accomplishment that has a distancing effect. The moralism of Girardian theory is equally, if not more, distancing. Salvation becomes thoroughly subjective: "It concerns only men's attitude to the Crucified, as if God's attitude to him did not exist."[3] To be sure, I recognize that language of "participation" and "identification" permeates Daniels's essay. In baptism and the Eucharist as the church's sacraments, we participate in Christ and in his body. The problem is that his participatory language is thoroughly at odds with the thought of Girard, whose quasi-Gnostic view of redemption as knowledge or awareness has no eye for participation in Christ.

Daniels may well be right that the contemporary evangelical emphasis on praise for an accomplished forensic salvation has a distancing effect. But for a remedy he would do better to turn to the broad Christian tradition than to Girard. Irenaeus's concept of recapitulation would be a good place to start. Such recapitulation implies that Christ—as the representative head of the new humanity—takes on the suffering and death that we deserve. This is a substitution of sorts—not one in which a transaction takes place in which we are not personally involved, but an inclusive substitution in which Christ as the Second Adam and as the New Israel takes on our humanity and so makes us share—participate—in all his benefits. Without such an inclusive substitution, union with Christ becomes an empty phrase. The Calvinist tradition may well have its shortcomings. But one of its most positive elements is surely a lively sense of union with Christ—a sharing or participation in the cross and resurrection of Christ.

Notes

1. René Girard, *I See Satan Fall Like Lighting*, trans. James G. Williams (Maryknoll, NY: Orbis, 2001), 32, 35, 70.
2. Hans Urs von Balthasar, *The Action*, vol. 4 of *Theo-drama: Theological Dramatic Theory*, trans. Graham Harrison (San Francisco: Ignatius, 1994), 309. With appreciation to my student Ryan Chace for pointing me to von Balthasar.
3. Ibid., 312.

Response to T. Scott Daniels
Thomas Finger

This author provides an excellent overview of Girard's approach, and creative suggestions for practicing baptism and the Lord's Supper. In my view, though, the "nonsubstitutionary" emphasis, even polemic, in his title and in much of the essay obscures these contributions somewhat. I find his first section weakest. Daniels claims that substitutionary themes pervade current evangelical worship; but he mentions only one song. From this one song he selects one phrase, "my debt to pay," as evidence of its "straightforwardly substitutionary" orientation.[1]

However, he overlooks the song's structure, which is clearly narrative: incarnation ("from heaven to earth"), life ("to show the way/ From the earth to the cross"), death ("the cross/my debt to pay"), descent to Hades ("From the cross to the grave"), and resurrection ("from the grave to the sky"). Those who sing are also "so glad You're in my life." "Lifting up," then, may not so much focus on "the sky," encouraging a "form of life" based on "distance,"[2] as extoling, in worship, the One present in their everyday existence.

Daniels faults substitution for omitting discipleship, or "radical redemptive participation in the world."[3] However, he misreads this model somewhat by focusing almost entirely on Jesus' death as the penalty for sin, and largely overlooking the importance of Jesus' life, where his obedience merited eternal life. Nevertheless, "obedience" is too abstract to capture those features of Jesus' life, including nonviolence, which make discipleship concrete. To be fair to what substitutionary theologians actually say, though, I find it better to critique the limitations of "obedience" than to imply that they ignore Jesus' life.

Girard's theory corresponds at many points with my appropriation of *Christus Victor*. However, I developed my view before hearing of Girard, and have never studied him in detail. Daniels makes a strong case that the cross manifested not divinely sanctioned violence (Boersma), but God's exposure of, and strong judgment upon, violence. God did not directly inflict judgment upon Jesus' killers. They drew that judgment upon themselves, precisely by participating in that violence. Our author considers God's judgment to be *indirect*, much as I do: "not so much God's direct and wrathful condemnation but . . . the result of human actions that fall down upon themselves."[4] As Romans 1 puts it, "God's 'wrathful' judgment is giving the creation up to its own desires."

Daniels rightly notes that "Girard's theory opens new possibilities for understanding Christ as *Christus Victor*"—though I am not sure that all these possibilities are new! Much like *Christus Victor*, he conceptualizes sin as two-sided. On one hand, humans participate in sin, for "we have rebelled against God." On the other, humans have also been bound by stronger Powers, and "'must be extracted from their own prison if they are to be capable of accepting the pure gift of freely offered love.'"[5] Perhaps, however, in contrast to me, our author prioritizes sin's systemic side by adding, "'We do not freely surrender our authenticity; it is stolen from us by the Powers.'"[6]

Daniels' assessment of Girard is almost wholly positive. Only in a footnote does he acknowledge that his theory includes speculation about prehistoric culture and may not apply to all kinds of sacrifice.[7]

One of Girard's contributions is "a way of interpreting the often embarrassing violence of the Old Testament as 'the residue of false ideas about God carried over from the general human past.'"[8] But since our author values biblical narrative, I wonder whether its progressive character might provide a stronger basis for some such critique (as he notices in the story of Gideon). Jesus clearly challenged some readings of the Old Testament. Daniels hopes to influence churches with a substitutionary outlook. How much can he draw on an anthropological theory that at points critiques the Bible?

Daniels applies his theology helpfully to sacramental practice. Baptism can certainly express identification with, and participation in, Jesus' life, death, and resurrection, as well as drowning sinful mimetic patterns. He appears to be referring chiefly, however, and perhaps exclusively, to believers' baptism.

Daniels seems to consider the Eucharist mainly a memorial of Jesus' death. It should indeed call us to "a particular kind of remembering," including awareness of our proclivity to violence. When he calls partaking of Jesus' body and blood "a mimetic practice," he again appears to accent the memorial function.[9] Daniels also stresses a communal dimension, but by means of an either/or: communion's focus "is not upon some magical, heavenly food but rather upon Christ and their brothers and sisters around the table."[10] Does Daniels restrict Eucharistic reality to the earthly, historical sphere? Or did Jesus actually ascend "from the grave to the sky"? If so, might he also be present in some empowering spiritual way?

Finally, Daniels rewrites the Lenten liturgy in either/or fashion. Well-known Scripture texts with their rhythmic cadence are replaced by a sociological kind of language. I fully affirm the content of this revision; but it brings nonviolence, gender, racial, and political concerns together much as educated liberals do. This may sound suspect to many members of many congregations. In worship might not it often be better to combine biblical language with other kinds of language (both/and), than to replace it with them?

Notes

1. Daniels, 128.
2. Ibid.
3. Ibid., 129.
4. Ibid., 133.
5. Ibid., 136 (quoting Schwager).
6. Ibid. (quoting Wink).
7. Ibid., 147, note 31 (following Wink).
8. Ibid., 134 (quoting Wink).
9. Ibid., 140.
10. Ibid.

BIBLIOGRAPHY

Aulen, Gustaf. *Christus Victor: An Historical Study of the Three Main Types of the Idea of the Atonement.* Trans. A. G. Hebert. London: SPCK, 1970.

Bailie, Gil. *Violence Unveiled: Humanity at the Crossroads.* New York: Crossroad, 1995.

Baker, Brenda M. "Penance as Model for Punishment." *Social Theory and Practice* 18 (1992): 311-31.

Bartlett, Anthony W. *Cross Purposes: The Violent Grammar of Christian Atonement.* Harrisburg, PA: Trinity, 2001.

Blocher, Henri. "*Agnus Victor:* The Atonement as Victory and Vicarious Punishment." In *What Does It Mean to Be Saved? Broadening Evangelical Horizons of Salvation,* edited by John G. Stackhouse, 67-91. Grand Rapids, MI: Baker Academic, 2002.

Boersma, Hans. "Eschatological Justice and the Cross: Violence and Penal Substitution." *Theology Today* 60 (2003): 186-99.

———. "Irenaeus, Derrida and Hospitality: On the Eschatological Overcoming of Violence." *Modern Theology* 19 (2003): 163-80.

———. *Violence, Hospitality, and the Cross: Reappropriating the Atonement Tradition.* Grand Rapids, MI: Baker Academic, 2004.

Brock, Rita Nakashima. *Journeys by Heart: A Christology of Erotic Power.* New York: Crossroad, 1988.

Brock, Rita Nakashima, and Rebecca Ann Parker. *Proverbs of Ashes: Violence, Redemptive Suffering, and the Search for What Saves Us.* Boston: Beacon Press, 2001.

Brown, Joanne Carlson. "Divine Child Abuse?" *Daughters of Sarah* 18, no. 3 (1992): 24-28.

Brown, Joanne Carlson, and Carole R. Bohn, eds. *Christianity, Patriarchy, and Abuse: A Feminist Critique.* New York: Pilgrim Press, 1989.

Brümmer, Vincent. *The Model of Love: A Study in Philosophical Theology.* Cambridge: Cambridge University Press, 1993.

Crysdale, Cynthia S. W. *Embracing Travail: Retrieving the Cross Today*. New York: Continuum, 1999.

Davis, Stephen T., Daniel Kendall, and Gerald O'Collins, eds. *The Redemption: An Interdisciplinary Symposium on Christ as Redeemer*. Oxford: Oxford University Press, 2004.

Fiddes, Paul. *Past Event and Present Salvation: The Christian Idea of the Atonement*. Louisville: Westminster John Knox, 1989.

Finger, Thomas. *A Contemporary Anabaptist Theology: Biblical, Historical, Constructive*. Downers Grove, IL: InterVarsity Press, 2004.

—————. "Biblical and Systematic Theology in Interaction: A Case Study on Atonement." In *So Wide a Sea: Essays in Biblical and Systematic Theology*, edited by Ben Ollengurger, 1-17. Elkhart, IN: Institute of Mennonite Studies, 1991.

—————. "Pilgram Marpeck and the Christus Victor Motif." *Mennonite Quarterly Review* 78, no. 1 (January 2004), 53-77.

Girard, René. *I See Satan Fall Like Lightning*. Trans. James G. Williams. Maryknoll, NY: Orbis, 2001.

—————. *The Scapegoat*. Trans. Yvonne Freccero. Baltimore: Johns Hopkins University Press, 1986.

—————. *Things Hidden Since the Foundation of the World*. Trans. Stephen Bann and Michael Metteer. Stanford: Stanford University Press, 1987.

—————. *Violence and the Sacred*. Trans. Patrick Gregory. Baltimore: Johns Hopkins University Press, 1977.

Gorringe, Timothy. *God's Just Vengeance: Crime, Violence and the Rhetoric of Salvation*. Cambridge: Cambridge University Press, 1996.

Green, Joel B., and Mark D. Baker. *Recovering the Scandal of the Cross: Atonement in New Testament and Contemporary Contexts*. Downers Grove, IL: InterVarsity Press, 2000.

Gunton, Colin E. *The Actuality of Atonement: A Study of Metaphor, Rationality and the Christian Tradition*. Grand Rapids, MI: Eerdmans, 1989.

Hamerton-Kelly, Robert G. *The Gospel and the Sacred: Poetics of Violence in Mark*. Minneapolis: Fortress Press, 1994.

—————. *Sacred Violence: Paul's Hermeneutic of the Cross*. Minneapolis: Fortress Press, 1992.

Hardin, Michael. "Violence: René Girard and the Recovery of Early Christian Perspectives." *Brethren Life and Thought* 37 (1992): 107-20.

Hill, Charles E., and Frank A. James, ed. *The Glory of the Atonement: Biblical, Historical, and Practical Perspectives: Essays in Honor of Roger Nicole.* Downers Grove, IL: InterVarsity Press, 2004.

Houts, Margo G. "Atonement and Abuse: An Alternative View." *Daughters of Sarah* 18, no. 3 (Summer 1992): 29-32.

Juergensmeyer, Mark, ed. *Violence and the Sacred in the Modern World.* London: Frank Cass, 1992.

Lefebure, Leo D. *Revelation, the Religions, and Violence.* Maryknoll, NY: Orbis, 2000.

————. "Victims, Violence and the Sacred: The Thought of René Girard." *Christian Century* 113 (December 11, 1996): 1226-29.

Mann, Alan. *Atonement for a "Sinless" Society: Engaging with an Emerging Culture.* Milton Keynes, UK: Paternoster-Authentic, 2005.

Marshall, Christopher D. *Beyond Retribution: A New Testament Vision for Justice, Crime, and Punishment.* Grand Rapids, MI: Eerdmans; Auckland: Lime Grove House, 2001.

McDonald, H. D. *The Atonement of the Death of Christ: In Faith, Revelation, and History.* Grand Rapids, MI: Baker, 1985.

McIntyre, John. *The Shape of Soteriology: Studies in the Doctrine of the Death of Christ.* Edinburgh: T & T Clark, 1992.

Milavec, Aaron. "Is God Arbitrary and Sadistic? Anselm's Atonement Theory Reconsidered." *Schola* 4 (1981): 45-94.

Milbank, John. *Being Reconciled: Ontology and Pardon.* London: Routledge, 2003.

Nessan, Craig L. "Violence and Atonement." *Dialog* 35 (1996): 26-34.

Paterson, Stephen J. *Beyond the Passion: Rethinking the Death and Life of Jesus.* Minneapolis: Fortress Press, 2004.

Peterson, David, ed. *Where Wrath and Mercy Meet: Proclaiming the Atonement Today.* Carlisle, Cumbria, UK: Paternoster, 2001.

Ray, Darby Kathleen. *Deceiving the Devil: Atonement, Abuse, and Ransom.* Cleveland: Pilgrim Press, 1998.

Schwager, Raymund. *Jesus in the Drama of Salvation: Toward a Biblical Doctrine of Redemption.* Trans. James G. Williams and Paul Haddon. New York: Crossroad, 1999.

————. *Must There Be Scapegoats? Violence and Redemption in the Bible.* Trans. Maria L. Assad. San Francisco: Harper & Row, 1987.

Sherman, Robert. *King, Priest and Prophet: A Trinitarian Theology of Atonement.* New York: T & T Clark, 2004.

Snyder, T. Richard. *The Protestant Ethic and the Spirit of Punishment*. Grand Rapids, MI: Eerdmans, 2001.

Suchocki, Marjorie Hewitt. *The Fall into Violence: Original Sin in Relational Theology*. New York: Continuum, 1994.

Swartley, Willard M., ed. *Violence Renounced: René Girard, Biblical Studies, and Peacemaking*. Telford, PA: Pandora, 2000.

Taylor, Mark Lewis. *The Way of the Cross in Lockdown America*. Minneapolis: Fortress Press, 2001.

Turner, H. E. W. *The Patristic Doctrine of Redemption: A Study of the Development of Doctrine During the First Five Centuries*. London: Mowbray; New York: Morehouse-Gorham, 1952.

Volf, Miroslav. *Exclusion and Embrace: A Theological Exploration of Identity, Otherness, and Reconciliation*. Nashville: Abingdon Press, 1996.

Weaver, J. Denny. "Atonement and the Gospel of Peace." In *Seeking Cultures of Peace: A Peace Church Conversation*, edited by Fernando Enns, Scott Holland, and Ann K. Riggs, 109-23. Telford, PA: Cascadia Publishing House; copublisher, Herald Press, 2004.

―――――. *The Nonviolent Atonement*. Grand Rapids, MI: Eerdmans, 2001.

―――――. "Violence in Christian Theology." *CrossCurrents* 51, no. 2 (Summer 2001): 150-76.

Westerhoff, Caroline. *Good Fences: The Boundaries of Hospitality*. Cambridge: Cowley, 1999.

Williams, Delores S. *Sisters in the Wilderness: The Challenge of Womanist God-Talk*. Maryknoll, New York: Orbis, 1993.

Williams, James G. *The Bible, Violence, and the Sacred: Liberation from the Myth of Sanctioned Violence*. Valley Forge: Trinity, 1995.

Wink, Walter. *Engaging the Powers: Discernment and Resistance in a World of Domination*. Minneapolis: Fortress Press, 1984.

Wright, N. T. *Jesus and the Victory of God*. Vol. 2 of *Christian Origins and the Question of God*. Minneapolis: Fortress Press, 1996.

―――――. *The Resurrection of the Son of God*. Vol. 3 of *Christian Origins and the Question of God*. Minneapolis: Fortress Press, 2003.

Subject Index

Abelard, Peter, xiv, 4, 6, 10, 33, 75, 89, 116, 136
Anselm, xiii, 3-8, 10, 12-14, 17, 23, 36, 43, 53, 73, 75, 89, 107, 109, 116, 160
apokatastasis, 52
atonement
  ahistorical, 9-10
  comprehensive meaning of, 88, 101, 103-4, 106
  dehistoricizing of, 49-50, 56, 64, 80
  juridicizing of, 49-50, 56, 64, 80, 89, 97-98, 101-3
  limited, 49, 66
  and passivity, 10, 12
  and resurrection, xi, xiii, 9, 12, 21, 25-27, 29, 35, 38, 48, 56, 65-66, 75, 95, 97, 101-3, 105, 110, 116, 121-22, 133, 137, 151-53
  theories of (*see Christus Victor*, moral influence, penal substitution, ransom, and satisfaction)
Augustine, 58, 61-63, 66, 68
Aulen, Gustaf, 89, 115

bantustans, 11
baptism, 62, 64, 69, 110, 126, 137-39, 148, 153-55, 157-58
Bartlett, Anthony, 129
Beker, J. Christian, 24
black theology, 10
Brock, Rita Nakashima, 11, 27-28, 47, 54, 66-67, 73
Brown, Joanne Carlson, 11

Caligula, 18
Calvin, John, xiv

Calvinism, 48-50, 53, 61, 63-64, 66-68, 156
capitalism, 13-14
catharsis, 131
child abuse, divine, 6-7, 15, 25, 33, 40, 47-48, 51, 99
Christus Victor theory of atonement, xiii, xvi, 2, 5, 12, 14, 17, 19, 21, 23-36, 33, 37-38, 40, 43-46, 51-52, 55-56, 73-75, 80-82, 84, 88-98, 101-5, 107, 109, 115-18, 121-22, 136, 151, 157-58
  as transformative and conflictive, 38, 101, 157-58
Clapp, Rodney, 138, 148
Claudius, 18
Collins, Robin, 129, 146
concursus, 33
Cone, James, 10, 11
Constantine, 10, 27-29, 36, 116
contagion, mimetic, 131, 154-55
cosmic battle, 2, 14, 17, 33, 92, 94, 102
Cur Deus Homo, 3-4, 12, 27, 107, 109
curse of the Law, 50, 55-56, 60, 80, 85
Cyril of Alexandria, 50-51

deception, divine, 52-53, 67, 80
Derrida, Jacques, 64, 69
deterrence, 58-60
devil. *See* Satan
disciple's cross, 126-29
Dodd, C. H., 120
Domitian, 17-18

Eucharist, 62, 64, 69, 126, 137-40, 153-55, 158-59
exclusion, divine, 49
exile, Babylonian, 38, 56, 58, 80-81, 85

SCRIPTURE INDEX